MUDRA THERAPY by Sabrina Mesk

MW00632767

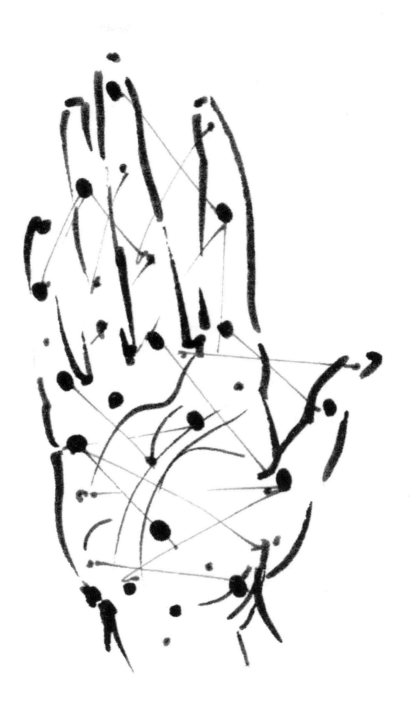

By Sabrina Mesko

Healing Mudras : Yoga for Your Hands - original Random House 2000
Power Mudras : Yoga Hand Postures for Women -original Random House

CHAKRA MUDRAS DVD's
HAND YOGA for Vitality, Creativity and Success
HAND YOGA for Concentration, Love and Longevity

HEALING MUDRAS
Yoga for Your Hands - New Edition 2013

HEALING MUDRAS - New edition in Full Color
Healing Mudras I. - For Your Body
Healing Mudras II. - For Your Mind
Healing Mudras III. - For Your Soul

MUDRAS FOR ASTROLOGICAL SIGNS 12 book set

POWER MUDRAS
Yoga Hand Postures for Women - New Edition

YOGA MIND
45 Meditations for Inner Peace, Prosperity and Protection

MUDRA THERAPY
Hand Yoga for Pain Management and Conquering Illness

MUDRA THERAPY

Hand Yoga for Pain Management
And Conquering Illness

Sabrina Mesko Ph.D.H

MUDRA THERAPY by Sabrina Mesko

The material contained in this book has been written for informational
purposes and is not intended as a substitute for medical advice nor is it
intended to diagnose, treat, cure, or prevent disease. If you have a
medical issue or illness, consult a qualified physician.

A Mudra Hands™ Book
Published by Mudra Hands Publishing

Photography by Mara
Illustrations by Kiar Mesko
Costume design, photo design, and styling by Sabrina Mesko
Cover photo by Mara
Cover and interior book design by Sabrina Mesko
Printed in the United States of America

ISBN-13: 978-0615879857
ISBN-10: 0615879853

For my Mother

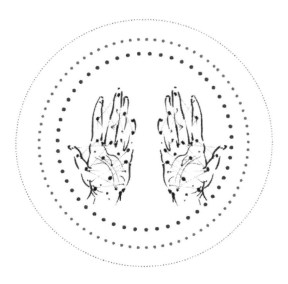

CONTENTS

PART 5: Mudra Therapy Sets for Specific Ailments

ACKNOWLEDGMENTS
My deepest gratitude goes to my Teacher Yogi Bhajan

MUDRA THERAPY

Hand Yoga for Pain Management
And Conquering Illness

Introduction

When I wrote my first book "Healing Mudras" that was published thirteen years ago, I had already spent many years practicing, teaching and continuously researching Mudras in private study with my teacher Yogi Bhajan. His wisdom was endless and he had such a clear vision and deep knowledge about my life and the work ahead, that it took my breath away at times. As years have gone by, I'm always aware when another one of his predictions manifests. And so it is that my work with Mudras continues to be one of my life's missions. I have been traveling, lecturing and educating about the power of Mudras, have worked individually and in groups with more students than I can recall, and I can honestly say that the results were always profoundly positive and most effective.

Mudras are sacred keys to empower, protect and heal your body, mind and spirit. When used properly, they transform your life.

At birth, each one of us received the gift of life, a physical body that is incredibly intricate and complex. But there is so much more to our body than we can't see with our own eyes. It is a fact, that in realms of subtle energy and the way it affects us on many levels, we still seem to know so little about. We are slowly coming into this new awareness and realization of how sensitive we truly are. I look forward to our evolution in the field of sound, color and all sensory healing arts.

However, in the area of touch, Mudras truly are a gem. Sometimes the most precious things in life are free - you do not need anyone else or any-thing to practice Mudras; just your hands and the knowledge how to use them. The rest happens on it's own.

Thru my years of working with Mudras with various clients, I have enjoyed observing first hand the deeper long term healing effects of these hand postures. I can't say it took me by surprise for I knew the profound effects and powerful transformation as a result of practicing this technique, but something else occurred. I realized that as time goes by, the readers needed ongoing instruction for very specific ailments in a way of a structured and systematic approach. I get continuously asked about best order and application of Mudra practice for conquering a very specific health challenge. I feel the time has come to offer this deeply therapeutic information in a book format, so that more practitioners can benefit from and have access to these ancient and powerful techniques.

There are many aspects needed to be able to enjoy great health. As our world presents more challenges with polluted environment, conventional food that many of us are allergic to, and electromagnetic over-saturation, we need to find more ways to protect ourselves. We need more information, more tools, more awareness and more discipline to stay healthy. This is not easy to come by. We are busier than ever, while at the same time we need more time to pay attention to all the details in order to simply stay healthy.

Long hours of meditation or exercise are unrealistic since we have less time than ever. That means we need quick steps, easy to understand tools, and affordable methods to help us along.

It's easy to say to someone who is suffering from a challenging illness to "just start leading a healthy lifestyle, be stress free, and eat right". But what is that specific lifestyle and healthy diet for that particular person? How can they transform their response to stressful circumstances? How can one take months to figure out why certain foods are damaging and inappropriate for their health? How much study can one do to understand all elements that should be changed or removed from their daily life? And how can one maintain a calm, peaceful demeanor when they are constantly bombarded with unharmonious vibrations all around them? Yes, we may eliminate some stressful aspects, but we all know too well that it is impossible to push a magic button and instantly eliminate all stress from your life. There are people, families, circumstances, work and countless stress triggering elements that are in our life permanently, and can not disappear overnight. That is not the realistic solution. Yes, anyone can feel better on a carefree vacation. That requires no mastery. But living day to day, dealing with life as it comes - that requires great discipline to manage. So the only thing we can effectively change is our response to a particular stressful circumstance. Maintaining inner calm and peace no matter what surrounds you - now that requires real mastery of mind! Healthy lifestyle involves also your home environment and personal dynamics. You can not expect to be healthy while living in a chaotic environment or in an unhappy relationship. This is also a kind of stress that takes its toll. And even when someone seems incredibly successful, that does not translate to a happy stress -free life. The visual impression of success matters little when you are unhappy. If you are unhappy you are not successful. If you ignore your health - you are not successful. One day when you least expect it, your physical body's health will challenge you, and force you to change everything about your life that you have been ignoring. Now you need directions, you need patience, you need tools to calm down, reassess the situation and figure out how to heal. Mudra Therapy is one of those tools. It's fairly easy to practice, it will help you with centering your inner core energy, hearing your inner voice, and controling your emotions, instead of letting them get the best of you. When you are able to maintain a healthy state of mind and emotions no matter what the circumstances, you have won. It's as easy as that - or as difficult.

Mudra Therapy will help you heal on physical, emotional, mental and subtle energy level.

The positive effects of Mudras are magnified when you create an optimal healing sensory environment for your Mudra practice. By soothing and energizing all your senses so that your body, mind and spirit are absorbing the powerful vibrations on many levels, the effects will be profound. It is under these circumstances that you can transcend your unharmonious state and regain healthy function.

Keeping your body, mind and emotions balanced will help you navigate thru the toughest of storms. You are stronger than any illness, if you know and are aware of all those intricate subtle energy dynamics that play a decisive role in your health. Whatever is not harmonious in your life has to be addressed and minimized. If you ignore it, the work required to repair the damage will be that much harder, longer and more challenging.

You have to outsmart your enemy-which is anything that brings you stress. First things first, so get to know yourself.

How do you really feel in this body, mind and heart? Acknowledge your state, don't just rush all day and night only to start again the next day.

This is your life and time is ticking. When you have an illness or are in pain, your whole life changes. Your illness requires your full attention - that is what pain is about. It is screaming "I am here, hear me, listen to me and figure me out!!"

Now you have two options: you can numb your body and continue like before, only to make matters worse. Or you can stop in your tracks right now and get to the very bottom of your challenge while honestly exploring your complete being; body, emotions, mind and utilize all your senses to regain your health. Your body wants to get healed and is programmed to do so. Your emotions are a bit trickier, but can be transformed. And then there is the biggest challenge of them all: your mind. BUT, you can tame that wild horse as well. Mudra Therapy addresses all those aspects and helps you re-program your life and yourself to your liking. And when you accomplish that, the world is a much better place and your life begins anew. Here is to you conquering all illness and establishing unbeatable, happy and healthy body, mind and spirit.

My blessings to you,
Sabrina

PART 1.

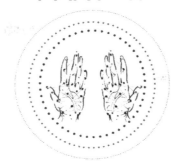

MUDRAS and ENERGY ANATOMY

WHAT ARE MUDRAS

Mudras are ancient healing hand gesture techniques that are practiced with your hands and fingers. They are yoga hand positions, symbolic gestures, a basic element of dance ritual and an integral part of religious ceremonies. Mudras originated in Egypt over 5000 years ago and can be found in every culture on Earth. The language of hand gestures knows no barriers of place and time.

HOW DO MUDRAS WORK

By placing your arms, hands and fingers in intricate specific positions, you can positively affect and improve your entire physical, emotional and mental state and your overall well-being. Mudras work by affecting your subtle energy body centers - chakras, and energy currents called nadis, as well as your brain centers. They help release and eliminate any blocked negative energy to promote a healthy, vibrant and regenerated energy flow. Mudras stimulate the immune system, balance the emotional state, increase mental receptivity and generally improve your overall health. Your fingertips are directly related to your consciousness and your engagement of fingertips is therefore your direct engagement with your consciousness.

WHAT IS MUDRA THERAPY

Mudra Therapy is a complementary non-invasive healing modality that can be used in any combination with traditional or alternative treatments, magnifying your receptivity to positive effects of other healing methods. Mudra Therapy facilitates your body's natural self-healing mechanism by addressing and eliminating various challenging aspects of your emotional, mental and physical health. Once the healthy energy flow is reestablished, your body can resume functioning in a healthy and balanced way.
In order for healing to occur, you need to clear the unseen deep subtle energy blockages that are causing disharmony and preventing you from enjoying a state of optimal health.

HOW DOES MUDRA THERAPY WORK

With a systematic use of hand yoga - Mudra positions combined with Sensory Holistic Healing techniques, you can effectively eliminate the source of your physical disharmony - and stimulate your body's natural self-healing mechanism. This process results in deeply therapeutic and regenerative effects and helps your body re-establish a state of balance. Mudras help you create an emotionally and energetically active self-healing environment so that you may enter a state of OPTIMAL HEALING RECEPTIVITY. Now the healing process can begin.

MUDRA THERAPY AS PREVENTATIVE MEASURE

Mudras can also be used as a preventative measure and a regular part of your daily healthy lifestyle practice or a disciplined wellness regimen. Maintaining your optimal health is possible when you consciously and regularly practice Mudras to help you deal with ongoing everyday issues that could, if left un-addressed, result in challenging emotional, mental and eventually physical health consequences.

By reducing the stress levels, releasing toxins, regenerating your body, and maintaining a peaceful, inner calm disposition - no matter what your environment or circumstances - you can overcome life's most challenging situations and remain healthy in body, mind, and spirit.

YOUR BODY FROM A HOLISTIC POINT OF VIEW

Holistic healing approach means that we take into consideration all aspects of your physical, psychological, emotional and mental states. Seeing your body as a whole complete system and a multidimensional intricate marvel, is a key component for profound and deeper insight, especially when addressing your health challenges. Every aspect of your being must be taken into consideration in order to find clues, causes and eventually answers to your pending health questions.

Your emotions play a critical role in your overall health dynamic and can greatly influence your general physical condition. Recognizing key emotional aspects in yourself will help you understand and correctly address the challenging health situations you may be facing.

Another decisive factor is your mindset, thinking habits, and patterns. Your mind and your thoughts are your ever-present companion and your mental disposition plays a large role in every aspect of your life and consequently your health.

Your subtle energy sensitivity to environment also influences all your daily dynamics. The ongoing daily energy exchange, energy receptivity and output - all of these elements affect you. Your energy body is never stagnant, but it continuously changes in response to each action, interaction, each thought and outside stimuli. Your body, your mind, your emotions - they are all a part of YOU.

When addressing any kind of ailment, health challenge, disharmony or illness, it is also essential that you observe every singular aspect of your immediate living environment. It is the complete synergy of all these elements that contribute to the final and complete picture of your overall condition.

You are the sum total of all these interconnected dynamics, not separated and dissected into thousands of singular parts. Another important aspect is to practice body awareness, consciously connecting to every physical part of you. Your toe is still your toe, it is connected to your entire body, all your energy currents are connected with that toe, your thinking patterns affect the toe, your living habits and your diet affect that toe - everything in some way or another affects the toe as well as every other cell in your body. And the wellness of your toe affects your entire state as well. A painful toe affects you emotionally, physically and mentally. You are one magnificent compilation of all these elements and when you realize the vastness of the details from your environment that affect your every singular cell, you will hopefully feel inspired to pay more attention to all these important key influences.

The reality is, that you can't expect to be healthy if certain areas of you and your life are completely ignored and deprived of proper attention.

You could practice yoga daily, but if your diet is unhealthy – your health regimen is incomplete.

If you do not address your emotional issues, your health regimen is still incomplete. If you remain ignorant about your thinking patterns that affect your daily disposition towards yourself, your work or relationships - the health regimen is again incomplete. If you don't make an effort to live in a healthy environment, all your other efforts for a healthy life-style will be less effective. It is an all or nothing game. Partial regimen for optimal health won't do.

Our current world is saturated with harmful substances, but fortunately it also offers many amazing remedies. It calls on you - to do your homework and actively participate. It requires paying attention to every detail of your life and taking responsibility for your decisions, actions and choices. One can't forever blame others for their current unhappy state and expect a miraculous positive change.

Living with awareness of each moment; this is a must. There are always a few choices you have, for nothing is written in stone. Have you given it some thought before you took on a new habit in your life? Have you reflected on your own, what is it that you need or want? Have you done some soul-searching or have you been putting it off, treating it as less important?

Nobody knows you as well as you can know yourself- have you looked within yourself? Have you listened to and acknowledged your deeper feelings? Have you asked yourself the basic questions about creating your happiness, finding your purpose and following your dreams? Or have you relied exclusively on decisions, recommendations and suggestions from others? Have you made choices in order to please others and fulfill someone's expectations? Have you decided to mute the inner voice and blind the inner vision in order to avoid facing your life's challenges?

If you want to feel happy and healthy on all levels of existence, you need to get to know yourself truly, deeply and in every aspect of your life. Pay attention to your thoughts, habits, tendencies, unresolved issues, dreams, desires, emotional states, weaknesses, urges, and every detail of your daily life. Live with awareness.

What do you want? Do you ever stop and hear your inner voice and the guidance from your subconscious that can provide you with those answers when you are calm and centered? Have you used all your capacities that are naturally given to you, to live the very best version of your life?

I know this seems like many questions, but a lot is at stake – you and the optimal version of your healthy and happy life.

The overall state of your physical body is the result of all your predispositions and consequent actions, lifestyle choices, unheard emotions and unresolved issues. Nobody is perfect. Yes, there are weaknesses one is born with, but that does not mean you can or should only be a helpless bystander in your own life. There is always movement in a positive direction that can be done - but that is up to you.

If you are ignoring certain prominent emotional or mental issues, your physical body will eventually force you to pay attention.

Physical, emotional, mental - all of those parts make the YOU.

What are your self-exploring habits? Do you endlessly chat on the phone with your friends while you are attempting self-analysis, do you practice stillness and reflect within, or do you simply ignore this issue? I encourage you to actively participate in the process of self-discovery and inner reflection. Your conscious participation will also be immensely valuable to any heath care professional that you may be working with and will help bring you closer to a solution of a problem. A good health care professional may have great counsel for you, but you are still the one that needs to take action. No one can do that instead of you. It takes discipline, effort, persistence, strength and self-love. Your wellness is a collaborative process, it is about you, not about passively accepting whatever comes your way. Be involved, observe, think, make an effort!

We usually pay attention only to the one obvious part of ourselves. The physical part. Why? Because, we live in a physical world and are less aware of our other subtler energy aspects. The subtle energy fields are physically invisible to us. If your visual capacity was such that you could observe your emotional and mental energy shifts in your body with your own eyes, you could see the negative effects and states that are continuously created as an immediate result of unbalanced lifestyle. But this way, since we cannot physically view those subtle energy states, we feel that: what we don't see, doesn't seem "real" and doesn't seem to matter. Our subtle energy state is hidden, unknown, secretive, mysterious, undiscovered and unaddressed.

Yet, it can be sensed, somewhat even seen, if you pay close attention and are focusing your receptivity on that level.

All of us have basic observation skills and by using them consciously we can improve and learn to truly pay attention to the world and people around us in a much wider, deeper and profoundly revealing way.

Now is the time to sharpen, awaken and begin using your deeper, penetrating, and all sensing observation powers. Your first project is you.

YOUR SUBTLE ENERGY BODY

Your energy body is much larger than your visible physical body - depending on numerous factors including your overall depleted or charged energy state and individual strength and presence. We are all different, and even in subtle realms we exist on various energy frequency levels. Your frequencies continuously change, however there is one frequency that is your dominant one. It may be lower – denser, or it may be finer-higher. This aspect makes no one better than the other. We are all humans, living this human experience and our finer subtle energy bodies reflect a fuller picture of who we are at this particular time and in this space. If you are meditating regularly and live a healthy conscious life, it does not mean that you are "better" than someone who is living an unhealthy lifestyle and suffering. It just means your experience is different, perhaps more fortunate since you are aware, alert and present. A person leading a life in unfortunate ignorance is absent. Often people who belong to certain thinking groups consider themselves above the rest, more spiritually evolved and better. As a result, they may look upon others with an attitude of superiority. And yet, a truly evolved spirit knows that a humble, respectful and compassionate non-judgmental disposition towards others who are less fortunate, less present or living in ignorance-is an essential part of evolutionary process. Feeling superior would indicate quite the opposite. Everyone has their own path. The life you live here and now is your path – your experience at this time. You have the good fortune to be alert, be present, and aware. Can you observe someone else with an open non-judgmental disposition and feel compassion for their ignorant state? Expand your awareness and be thankful for all you are, all you have, all you can and all you will do.

What we will learn in next chapters are various ways for recognizing character patterns that will help you understand the specific chakra energy level you are generally functioning at. This is truly fascinating. It is very helpful when observing yourself as well as others, and will help you gain a deeper understanding of the human condition.

The main energy frequency of your energy bodies as relating to chakras have many other aspects and subtle layers that reflect the different parts of you - the interesting invisible parts of you that are nevertheless all intricately interconnected.

Your subtle energy body is extremely sensitive to every aspect of your life. If you adjust your environment and surround yourself with sensory healing elements you will create profoundly positive circumstances for reestablishing a state of optimal health.

It is also important to note that your subtle energy body is your first line of defense- if you are in an unharmonious environment or surrounded by negative people, your energy body will create a protective shield and send you a message, an uneasy feeling seemingly for no reason. It will attempt to guide you to remove yourself from the circumstances and be cautious. If you are "in tune" you will be able to register this sensation or "intuitive feeling" and protect yourself in time. If you are emotionally overwhelmed, mentally unfocused or otherwise impaired, this hidden "warning capacity" will be impaired. It is most beneficial to be present, aware and take advantage of all subtle messages your energy body is transmitting.

AURA

Your body is an amazing structure of electromagnetic energy vibrations. Your aura - the large and invisible energy field around your body, is very receptive and sensitive to the vibrations of your environment. Sound, color, light, emotions, food, animals, flowers and all elements of nature affect your energy field. Other people, your interactions with them and changing environments continuously affect your aura. For example; when you are in a happy environment, filled with love and surrounded by your favorite harmonious and loving people, music and colors, your aura expands and glows stronger. If you find yourself in dangerous or uncomfortable situations, or are hurt and angry, your aura will instantly reflect a more contained and protective energy filed. The key to a physically healthy state is awareness and continuous care to assure your auric field stays as harmonious, clear, and strong as possible.

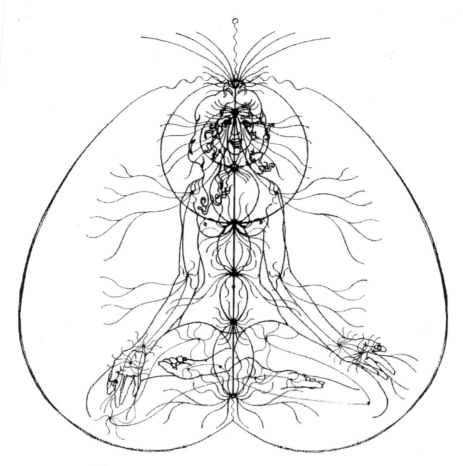

Chakras and Nadis in your energy body

PROLOGED NEGATIVE EFEFCTS ON AURA

If you continuously and for an extended period of time live in an unbalanced, unhappy environment, and lead an unhealthy lifestyle, consuming unhealthy food, your Aura will be less vibrant. If you abuse your body with drugs, smoking and or alcohol you will substantially weaken your auric protection field, making it easily penetrable and very vulnerable to undesirable influences and negative forces. Negative people, environments and addictions will overpower you and make you more susceptible to manipulation and uncontrollable unhealthy behavior. If you continue on this path, your auric field could be permanently damaged. Your own energy frequency will weaken and become desensitized to finer- higher frequencies. It will resonate more easily with negative aspects of lower plane frequencies that are coarse. As a result, it will become more challenging for you to keep your own power, make your own conscious decisions and be in charge of your actions. Your emotional state will be unpredictable, out of control, your mental state confused, unclear and out of focus. Your addictive desires will override any and all other needs, hopes and wishes. Your physical body will suffer various long term damaging effects of your unhealthy lifestyle that will trigger bad diet habits, dehydration, oxygen deprivation, disturbed sleeping patterns or too much exposure to disturbing electromagnetic fields. The out of balance addictive behavior will trigger disruptive and damaging consequences in all areas of your life. As a result your confidence will diminish, your insecurities will take charge and you may find yourself in a vicious cycle that proves challenging to break free of.

It is essential that you are clearly aware of these bad consequences when embarking on a self-destructive path. These negative effects seem invisible at first when they are damaging your energy body, but later the damaging effects will manifest in your physical body as well. Remember, your given physical constitution is also a factor and if someone else seems to be handling same destructive actions better, there is no guarantee that you will be able to sustain them the same way.

It is important to mention that also over-medicated states negatively affect your energy state and aura. Any excess will weaken and damage your delicate energy field. Unhealthy substances can stay in your subtle energy system for a very long time and will permanently damage the state of your energy field. It is never too late to break a bad pattern and redirect yourself on a new healthy and conscious path in life. Every day is a new beginning.

THE CHAKRAS AND CORRESPONDING CHARACTERISTICS

The seven main chakras are your core subtle energy centers. They are energy vortexes along your spine turning in a clockwise direction. In addition, you also have a chakra in each palm of your hand and in the soles of your feet. Chakra energy centers are extremely sensitive to outside stimuli and change constantly. They affect your entire physical, emotional, mental and spiritual well-being.

A simple unharmonious event that frightens or upsets you, creates an immediate reaction in your chakras, causing them to close off and function at a reduced capacity. Repetitive disturbing behavior will cause a chakra to become congested with dense negative energy matter, creating disharmony and preventing it from properly functioning. Any outside stimuli that challenges your inner peace has a negative effect on your charkas. On the other hand, a positive stimuli that promotes a healthy balance and inner stillness will help open, reactivate and properly spin your charkas with vibrant life force.

We are much more sensitive than we realize and everything affects us profoundly. Some of us seem less sensitive than others. If you consciously develop your senses, they are heightened. If you habitually dull the senses, you are out of touch – you can't properly access and receive the information that your senses could otherwise provide. It is important to note, that you are generally more comfortable in sensory environments that suit your dominant energy frequency.

If a person feels most comfortable with outside stimuli connected to the first chakra, it means they function mostly in that energy field - as that is their dominant energy level. Such a person will be less receptive to fourth chakra sensory elements and will not experience the sensory aspects in the same way as a person who is functioning mostly on fourth chakra energy level.

Additionally, a person who is depleted in their first chakra field will react differently to sensory experience connected to that chakra, even if they generally function at another chakra energy level. It is most important that we learn how to balance all our charkas, because a depleted chakra will most likely create an unbalance or energy overload in other chakras. Wherever you are experiencing negative energy in relation to corresponding governing chakra issues, you are creating an energy cluster of unhealthy vibration. Releasing and detoxifying that negative energy is necessary to promote healthy chakra function. Maintaining your optimal state of health is closely related to healthy function of your chakra subtle energies.

This is of course a simplified explanation for a quite intricate system, nevertheless it is important to be aware of and understand these basic aspects. It will help you understand yourself and your likes, dislikes, comfort zone and actions better. For a deeper understanding of the chakra system, we will review the basic chakra energy level characteristics and corresponding emotional states. Your energy state is always changing, however each one of us generally functions on one main frequency level. Each frequency reflects your overall character and ongoing character tendencies. Unbalance in a specific chakra creates challenging issues associated with that energy level. For example: If you are experiencing a challenging situation in matters of love, your 4th chakra will be out of alignment. Focusing on empowering the 4th chakra will help you stabilize the chakra and all matters of the heart. On some level an unharmonious condition in any chakra affects all other charkas as well.

FIRST CHAKRA
REPRESENTS: Survival, food, shelter, courage, will, vitality, foundation
LOCATION: Base of the spine
COLOR: Red
GLAND: Gonads
SENSE : Smell
SENSE ORGAN: Nose
ELEMENT: Earth
DESIRE: Security
CHALLENGES: financial security, awareness, inner strength, illusion, anger, greed, delusion, excess sensuality, basic fear of death, violent behavior based on insecurity, loss of basic security and fear.

SECOND CHAKRA
REPRESENTS: Creativity, sex, procreation, family, inspiration,
LOCATION: Sexual organs
COLOR: Orange
GLAND : Adrenal
SENSE: Taste
SENSE ORGAN: Tongue
ELEMENT: Water
DESIRE: Sexuality, family
CHALLENGES: restlessness, confusion, anxiety, over activity, emotions rule, emotional sensitivity to moon fluctuations, hunting, trickery, daydreaming, pro-creation

THIRD CHAKRA
REPRESENTS: Ego, emotional center, the intellect, the mind
LOCATION: Solar plexus
COLOR: Yellow
GLAND: Pancreas
SENSE : Sight
SENSE ORGAN: Eyes
ELEMENT: Fire
DESIRE: Immortality, authority, name, fame
CHALLENGES: Pride, vanity, control thru anger, power, recognition, selfishness, fear

FOURTH CHAKRA

REPRESENTS: Unconditional true love, devotion, faith, compassion
LOCATION; Heart
COLOR: Green or pink
GLAND; Thymus
SENSE : Touch
SENSE ORGAN: Skin
ELEMENT: Air
DESIRE: Love, faith, devotion, duty
DOMINANT CHARACTERISTICS: lives in harmony within inner and outer world, happy person, youthful, aware of life's actions and karma, striving to achieve balance, clarity of conscience

FIFTH CHAKRA

REPRESENTS: Voice, truth, communication, higher knowledge
LOCATION: Throat
COLOR: Blue
GLAND: Thyroid
SENSE : Hearing
SENSE ORGAN: Ears
ELEMENT: Ether
DESIRE: Knowledge
DOMINANT CHARACTERISTICS;
Voice penetrates to the heart of the listener, changing space and mind of the listener, distracting nature of the world no longer a problem, supreme reasoning, seeking only true knowledge

SIXTH CHAKRA

REPRESENTS: Third Eye, vision, intuition
LOCATION; Third Eye
COLOR: Indigo
GLAND: Pineal
DESIRE: Realization, clairvoyance, intuition
DOMINANT CHARACTERISTICS
Subtle energy light around head and aura, breath and mind under control, yogi in samadhi, capacity for vision from past, present and future, experiences clear perceptions, realization of immortal spirit in temporary body, duality is gone, reveals divinity within others, there is no danger of spiritual reversal, in his presence all become calm and sensitive, all duality is gone.

SEVENTH CHAKRA
REPRESENTS: Universal God consciousness, the heavens, unity, humility
LOCATION: Top of the head, crown
COLOR: Violet
GLAND: Pituitary
DESIRE: Union
DOMINANT CHARACTERISTICS : All feelings, emotions and desires are dissolved, the yogi is in Samadhi, a state of pure bliss and unity

CHAKRAS IN YOUR HANDS AND FEET
Besides the seven charkas that run along your spine, you also have a chakra in each foot and in each palm of your hand. The chakras in your feet are your receptors for feeling grounded and connected to the Earth. Walking barefoot in the grass or on the beach will instantly reconnect your with the healing power of nature and help revitalize your body. A foot massage is most beneficial for these chakras.
The chakras in your hands relate to giving and receiving. Your hands are sensitive receptors and the hand chakras can be easily stimulated by healing environments like fresh running water, touching the earth, petting an animal and of course positive human interaction. Pay attention to who you shake hands with and what you touch. A handshake is a powerful exchange of energy and if you intuitively do not feel like greeting a person this way - listen to your intuition and respect that. Hands are also great sensory "scanners" and can help you sense an energy blockage.
The way hands are used in Mudra Therapy is most important as they serve as connectors and conduits of energy. By placing hands in specific positions, you reconnect and activate nadis and help re-open and reactivate closed-off or less active main chakras. Your hand chakras are profoundly stimulated and empowered during Mudra Therapy practice.

THE NADIS
Your body has a network of seventy-two thousand electric currents called nadis. They run throughout your body from your toes to the top of your head and out to your fingertips. These channels of energy must be clear and vibrant with life force for your optimum health and empowerment. Your aura expands beyond your physical body and within this energy field are other smaller subtle chakras linked with nadis. There are two types of nadis: gross – as cords and vessels, and subtle - as invisible channels and conduits of subtle prana force and mental force.

THE SUBTLE ENERGY BODIES

The layers of your finer energy body's vibrations that surround and interlace with your physical body each reflect a specific part of you. These layers of your energy bodies are interconnected and interwoven. They are not separately expanding layers, but they occupy the same space at the same time – but they differ in frequency level. There are many different approaches and theories about the number of energy bodies, in Mudra Therapy it is important to be familiar with the basic seven layers that correspond with the seven main chakras.

Chakra One - The Etheric – physical - Body
Chakra Two -The Emotional body
Chakra Three – The Mental Body
Chakra Four - The Astral Body
Chakra Five - The Etheric Template
Chakra Six -The Celestial Body
Chakra Seven -The Casual Body

A healthy physical body does not necessarily mean that your emotional and mental energy bodies are healthy as well. Disease first manifests in your finer energy body layers; for example when unhappy emotions are present in your emotional energy body - if not resolved, their energy becomes denser and denser, eventually manifesting into physical illness. Similarly, a negative mental disposition that consistently exists in your mind and on your mental energy level, can eventually manifest into a physical illness. Fear of specific illness that one mentally dwells on, repeating and affirming they will suffer from it - this specific illness could manifest. Thoughts have power, every word or mental affirmation is made of frequencies that carry information. By keeping all your energy bodies clear of negative energy, you are preventing disease from manifesting and can successfully preserve your state of optimal health.
Be mindful and aware of your thoughts and spoken words.

YOUR HANDS AND THE SOLAR SYSTEM

Your body's subtle energy layers are also under the influence of our solar system. The right side of the body is ruled by the Sun and reflects the male qualities of your personality and is connected to your father and male figures in your life. It also signifies how strong you are in your male nature- regardless if you are a man or a woman. It is connected to your logic, mental functioning, practicality, willpower and determination

The left side of your body is ruled by the Moon and reflects the feminine side of your personality, and is connected to your mother and female figures in your life. It reflects your emotional expression, feelings, gentleness, and creative projects.

With the Mudra practice you are reconnecting the nadis of feminine and masculine qualities and energies and creating a balance and harmony within the physical, emotional and mental aspects of your being.

In addition, each of your fingers is specifically influenced by a planet.

THE THUMB
Ruled by Mars, reflects your willpower, logic and ego

THE INDEX FINGER
Ruled by Jupiter, reflects knowledge, justice, truth, honor, self confidence

THE MIDDLE FINGER
Ruled by Saturn, reflects patience, emotional control, ambition

THE RING FINGER
Ruled by the Sun, reflects vitality, health, love aspects

THE LITTLE FINGER
Ruled by mercury, reflects spoken and written communication, beauty, creativity

PART 2.

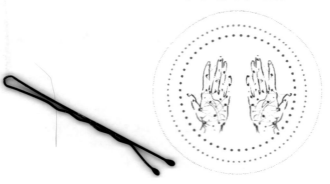

YOUR HEALTH

UNDERSTANDING YOUR CURRENT STATE OF HEALTH

In the following chapters you will learn about various aspects that have a direct effect on your current state of health. Read with attention to detail and specifically take note of elements that describe your current state. The intention here is to take you step by step thru the process of self-assessment where you can honestly observe your habits, emotional and mental dispositions, your lifestyle and all aspects of your everyday life. This is the first essential key step in your process of healing.

Once you acknowledge and accept responsibility for your contributing role in your current unharmonious condition, you can then consciously take charge and implement necessary changes to improve and eliminate your challenging health issues. If you feel that life's difficult circumstances that are out of your hands have contributed to your illness, I compassionately say: you still can improve your health. How? By changing your current state of helplessness, which is a negative mindset. And by changing your current emotional state of -perhaps anger in regards to misfortune that happened to you - which is a negative emotional aspect. Fight tough circumstances back the same way - with a tough disposition and determination for victory, which is a positive mental state. Emotionally, replace anger with self-love and gentle kindness to your body, again a positive emotional state. You must and will win. Persevere and don't give up – consciously direct your emotions and mind to work for you and not against you. Now, you are in charge, no matter what surrounds you.

YOUR CELLULAR IMPRINT

Each one of us is unique and a sum total of our many lives and experiences. Every single event that happened in your life up until now, left an energy imprint on your cells. Nothing goes unnoticed. A traumatic event may follow you for an entire lifetime and even if your life seems completely careless and free, in your core you still carry memories of this past event. If this memory and the connected emotional issues are unresolved, old trauma can prevent you from enjoying life in the present. Your cellular energy imprint also contains far memories from your past lifetimes. Certain emotionally unresolved far-past memories can carry over into today and continuously present an obstacle.

Similarly like emotional memories, physical challenges from past can also leave a cellular imprint in your energy body's memory and carry over into the present. If for example you endured a traumatic incident or injury in the far past, you may experience chronic pain in that specific area of your body even today- for no apparent reason.Often you may completely forget about an incident even from our childhood, but it is stored in your cellular memory. On a positive note, your uplifting and empowering experiences from your far past can also contribute to your current deeper knowledge, or courageous, confident or wise disposition. A deep sense of trusting the universe and the protection it provides can also stem from the knowledge gained from past lives. Inner peace and faith are grounded in your higher consciousness and the deep memory of your soul. The sooner you learn how to access your deep inner knowledge and power, the better, easier, happier and more fulfilled your life will be. Releasing the source of obstacles connected with unresolved past cellular memories is important and can be achieved with self-awareness, positive affirmations and by consciously releasing the blocked emotional energy connected with specific event or circumstance that caused it. Obviously, past life trauma that carries over into this lifetime needs in-depth work, often through regression therapy. Difficult events from your current life can be released with various healing modalities. How would you identify an emotionally challenging cellular imprint from the far past? An example would be an unexplained deep-set fear of loosing a person close to you, when there is no apparent reason for concern. Another case would be for a very successful person who is financially very secure experiencing crippling fear of lacking security– again, for no apparent logical reason. When emotions that prevent you from enjoying life at this present moment are completely disconnected with your current reality and situation, your trauma goes far back into your past. If there is absolutely no reason from your current life's past to justify or explain this deep set fear, then you can assume the source comes from your far away past. The key is deeply exploring your life, the dynamic with your parents and the patterns that were in your close environment when you were growing up. All those elements contributed to your current emotional and mental make-up. All these possibilities will hopefully inspire you to delve deeper into your psyche and explore every nuance of you and your state today.

WHAT IS A HEALTHY LIFESTYLE?

A healthy lifestyle is the key component for a disease-free body and mind. It encompasses much more than a healthy diet, exercise and body care. It involves every aspect of your entire physical, mental and emotional life. That means in addition to taking optimal care of your physical self, it is important to have a healthy mental disposition and awareness of your emotional states. Mudra therapy addresses all these aspects and helps you understand and consciously maintain an optimal all encompassing healthy lifestyle.

THE EFFECTS OF YOUR PSYCHOLOGICAL STATE ON CHAKRAS

YOUR EMOTIONS - CHAKRA 1 THROUGH 5

Your emotional state is a decisively important element of your energetic constitution and overall health. Emotions are affected by your hormones, nervous system, personality and your reactions to environment, events, other people, life experiences and various sensory stimuli. Holding on to unhappy emotions affects every aspect of your life. It is in your subtle emotional body where disharmony and disease appear before manifesting in your physical body. Whatever negative emotion you are experiencing, you can find the corresponding chakra that is affected. This self-exploring process will help you understand where in your physical and energy body you most likely have an energy blockage. This is very beneficial for you to understand while exploring which emotions help or hinder you. Your past negative experiences created certain dynamics or situations that you are emotionally over-sensitized about. This will prompt and trigger a bigger negative emotional reaction whenever you are in a similar situation. With Mudra Therapy method you can consciously begin shifting your emotional pre-dispositions, resulting in an overall better, happier, and healthier quality of life.

FIRST CHAKRA CENTER

If your emotional issues are connected with the will to live, financial, survival or existential concerns and shortcomings - it is your first chakra that will be most challenged. If these problems stay unresolved, health issues in that region could manifest. This most often happens to individuals that have endured years of struggle and stress with finances and livelihood. This can manifest in ailments of your lower spine, problems with elimination and general state of vitality. By selecting Mudra Therapy techniques to cleanse and strengthen the first chakra center, you will maintain your physical health in that region despite ongoing challenges.

SECOND CHAKRA CENTER

If your negative emotions are connected to your sexuality or unexpressed or ignored desire for creativity, your second chakra will suffer. If not addressed, you could develop numerous health issues connected to your reproductive organs. This is most often the case with people who live in an unhappy partnership and have created an invisible energy blocking barrier to avoid closeness and sexual contact. This is very unhealthy. The protective energy blockage eventually manifests in physical body as various ailments of reproductive system. Women are more vulnerable in this aspect, because they are more often silent about their negative emotions towards their partner, and are on the receiving end and more passive in this particular energy exchange process. When these issues remain unaddressed, they may experience challenges with ovaries, period cycles and fertility. Men who live in an unbalanced dynamic in this aspect of the relationship with their partner, often experience prostate issues. Using Mudra Therapy's natural healing techniques for balance of energy in second chakra center, will help you preserve health in that region.

THIRD CHAKRA CENTER
If your negative emotions are connected to fear, anger or ego issues, it is your third chakra that is challenged. This can manifest in various physical forms like ulcer and stomach or digestive problems. It also causes weight gain in that region - as invisible energy protection barrier that with time manifests in physical form of an expanded waist area. Learning how to release and eliminate this negative emotional energy cluster is essential. This chakra is also the last of the lower charkas, and by being able to lift your main frequency to the heart center, you enter a new level. In order to achieve that and remain healthy, you need to release all toxic emotions that may linger here– this chakra center needs much attention. Proper Mudra Therapy breathing from solar plexus is essential and most beneficial and healing.

FOURTH CHAKRA CENTER
If your negative emotions are connected to matters of the heart- like love, broken heart, lack of love, loss of love, grief, longing etc. eventually your heart region - fourth chakra will suffer consequences. This can often manifest in the form of incapacity to receive love, breast cancer, heart or lung problems. It is all about your heart and the sorrow, pain or emptiness that overwhelms it with energy blockages. You can eliminate this negative stuck energy by regularly cleansing and detoxifying your heart chakra region of pent-up emotions. Mudra Therapy sequences for health of this chakra will help you maintain optimal chakra functioning.

FIFTH CHAKRA CENTER
If your negative emotions have to do with the aspect of verbal arguments, bad communication, not speaking your mind, or repetitive chatter, and incapacity to verbally present yourself to the world, it will be your fifth chakra that will endure a challenge. This can be seen in personal relationship situations where one partner never speaks their mind about past or even current hurtful event and keeps everything inside, pent-up for

eternity. Dysfunctional communication, and unspoken words hurt you more than you can imagine. Unexpressed emotions stay stuck within your energy body. In health aspect this can result in vulnerability, loss of voice, chronic throat inflammation, trouble with neck, teeth, mouth and jaw. By consciously working on releasing the energy block, you can protect this energy center. Selecting Mudra Therapy for releasing blockages connected to this center will be most beneficial.

YOUR MENTAL DISPOSITION – CHAKRAS 6 AND 7

Your mind-computer has truly amazing powers. It can help you navigate thru life experiences and can be your greatest ally or your greatest enemy. Why? If your inner monologue is positive, encouraging, patient and loving you can overcome almost anything. But if your inner conversation is that of continuous discouragement and self-criticism and negative projection for all your efforts, your life will manifest accordingly. Controlling your mind and thoughts is beyond important, for no matter where you go, no matter what you do - your mind's voice is always with you. This inner conversation is going on all the time. Are you just passively participating in this one sided monologue or are you involved in a dialogue, participating and actually paying attention to what is being silently spoken in your mind? Who's voice is that? Is it from your distant past engrained in your memory and you never bothered to replace it?

 When you wake up in the morning; what is your first thought, how encouraging and supportive is this inner voice? If you are overwhelmed with emotional issues it will be very challenging to be in tune with your inner vision, as your unresolved emotions will prevent this from happening. Mudra Therapy will help you regain the power of your mind.

SIXTH CHAKRA CENTER

If your negative emotions substantially weaken any of your charkas below the sixth, you will experience weakness in this center. This chakra is more affected by your mental state and less by your emotions. The consequences will be a weakened intuition, visualization or understanding of mental concepts, obsessive thinking, inability to relax, and incapacity to focus on one subject. This can most often manifest in physical ailments like headaches, dizziness, various vision problems, and general difficulty with concentration. By applying Mudra therapy aspects for your mindfullness, you will be able to train and maintain your mind in a state of inner peace and calm. Your emotions however, must be balanced first.

SEVENTH CHAKRA CENTER

If your mind is incapable of exploring spiritual aspects of life and you feel challenged about the sense of self within society and your purpose, your seventh chakra is less vibrant than desired. First you need to address the emotional issues which are preventing your life force from equally vibrating through all your lower energy centers within your body. With Mudra Therapy you will systematically balance your centers one by one and eventually find the kind of inner balance to be able to extend your perception and observe various concepts of spirituality to find whatever brings you greatest level of strength, understanding and inner contentment.

In conclusion, I hope it is clearly reflected how interconnected all your chakra centers are, and if any center is not functioning properly, the next one and all consecutive ones will suffer with weakness. The more unresolved issues you have, the less energy will travel upward into the next energy center and depletion will affect every center. Now it becomes clear why a person overburdened with emotions of fear, can't expect to have a great intuition, or a person suffering in love, may not be able to speak about it at all. The combinations are truly endless, but once the energy obstacles are minimal, your optimal functioning will resume, the energy will flow properly and you will feel a decisive difference in every aspect of your life.

YOUR BREATHING PATTERNS

There is a direct link between conscious breathing, electrochemical balance of your brain and your nervous system.
Your breathing is absolutely essential and necessary for your survival. Your life starts with your first breath and ends with your last breath. What happens in between is your entire life. Your emotional state is closely connected to your breathing patterns, as they directly affect each other. If you feel frightened - your breathing changes. If you are joyful, happy - your breath adapts.The good news is, that the same principle works the other way around as well: your breathing pattern also affects your emotions. That means that by consciously changing your breathing pattern, you can positively affect and improve your emotional state. And that is truly fantastic news - it means that you can transform stressful, upsetting emotional states simply by mindfully changing your breathing pattern.

We all breathe perfectly as babies. Baby's chest expands when inhaling and relaxes and contracts when exhaling. You can observe that perfect peaceful breathing pattern when watching a sleeping baby. So what happens, why do we as grown ups breathe quite the opposite way? Inhaling while pulling our shoulders up and struggling to pull the stomach in? Your breathing changes as a result of emotional experiences mainly connected to anger or fear. When you get frightened, the stomach area cramps and tightens up, you are almost holding your breath. In case of anger, it is the same physical area that becomes tense. If we are less physically active we loose touch with our abdomen and breathe mostly with upper lungs. If we gain weight this only worsens our bad breathing habit. If we have a lot of unresolved and pent up emotions, this creates an energy blockage in our solar plexus as well as stomach area and not much healthy energy movement occurs there. Another factor for our incapacity for relaxed breathing in stomach region, also comes from social expectations promoting a tight firm stomach area. There is nothing wrong with a fantastic looking trimmed stomach, but often the exercise regimen to achieve that look does not include proper breathing or developing your capacity for relaxing and expanding the stomach as well. The focus is on tightness of stomach and not flexibility and suppleness. It is important to be aware that most of your body's release of toxins happens thru breathing - precisely exhalations. Your inhalation provides oxygen which is a big enemy of most diseases. The extra oxygen in your system increases your body's ability to destroy disease. Isn't that enough of a reason to breathe properly?

Holding your breath while working out is not beneficial. Breathing that is coordinated with each and every exercise movement is necessary and helps you exercise better.

Your usual breathing pattern reflects your overall emotional and mental state. If your breathing is shallow, you won't be able to truly deeply relax. If you breathe by mostly exhaling without a proper deep inhalation, you won't be upbeat and full of energy. A balanced strong inhale and equally strong exhale is needed for optimal breathing benefits.

There are mainly two types of breathing groups we all loosely fit into. Some of us are the "inhalers" and others are the "exhalers".

The inhalers are those who breathe mostly with inhalations and never truly deeply exhale. Such people are restless, very active, anxious, impatient and often very stressed. They exhale properly only towards the end of the day when they are completely exhausted. Many of us fall into this category. There is a seemingly positive side to this breathing habit- you will be active, you will get things done, your will seem like an endless bundle of energy. But in reality you will be too stressed and only running on half a steam. Imagine, if you would learn to balance your breathing properly - you would still have all the energy, but without restlessness, you would be able to pace yourself better and enjoy a complete moment of stillness amidst chaos around you. Stillness can be a very empowering state. Everything works better in stillness - your emotions are balanced, your observation skills fine tuned and your mind alert and fast. When you are living without being able to experience this stillness, all these capabilities are compromised.

The exhalers are of course the exact opposite. They start the day with a long exhalation and pretty much keep it that way for the rest of the day. About half of us belong to this group. Exhalers usually move much slower, they have less enthusiasm for new ventures and new ideas, they seem to be more stagnate, sleepy, substantially less optimistic and can always find a reason why something should not be done. They are able to sit still, but that does not equate stillness. They will sit without focus and alertness, their life force is low, their mind is in a haze and they could be in a repetitive thinking pattern resulting void of a single idea or solution. Inhaling vibrant life force is necessary and essential. When an exhaler finally learns to breathe properly, they feel dizzy with all the oxygen suddenly accessing areas of their brain, that were up until now functioning only on "fumes" since their "oxygen tank" was so low. With proper inhalations their disposition changes, they are overwhelmed with all the things they want to accomplish and projects they want to do. All this was in them, but in a dormant state waiting to be awoken on a destined day. As you see, when you learn to breathe properly, your life truly becomes different — you are connected and an alert participant on your life's journey.

The positive effects of healthy breathing are endless. Providing your body with oxygen is like providing it with the cleanest of energy sources — it cleanses, detoxifies, heals and rejuvenates your cells and your energy body. The negative effects of poor breathing habits are unfortunately equally extensive; depression, illness, passivity, loss of willpower only to name a few. Observe yourself and your breathing patterns - do you inhale deeply and from your solar plexus area? Are you struggling and lifting your shoulders? Learn the basics of proper breathing in the Mudra Therapy instruction section of this book and practice it every day until it becomes like second nature to you.

YOUR DIET

The days of careless eating are gone. The food is not the same as it was thirty, twenty or even ten years ago and today proper healthy nutrition requires some effort and right decisions. Not having enough time or energy to pay attention to your diet is not an acceptable excuse. Food is as essential as air and your daily awareness of what nourishes your body is a must. There are many seemingly very attractive foods out there that you can see in every commercial and advertising add – but chances are, a lot of them are unhealthy. Fast food is so void of proper fresh organic nutrients that it seems appetizing only with colorful packaging and mass advertising.

A healthy eating habit comes down to awareness, discipline and self-control. Just as unhealthy food, the proper healthy food is also easily available, you just need to pay attention and truly consciously select what you eat. You can find organic vegetables, organic cruelty free meats and gluten free products everywhere. If you shop locally at farmers markets you will find fresh vegetables that are organic, clean and healthy. If you ignore these important dietary aspects, it will catch up with you eventually. Wherever lies the weakness in your physical constitution, the bad nutrition will create and magnify negative consequences. That means that it is most beneficial and truly necessary to take some time and reestablish new eating habits that will help you remain in your optimal healthy state.

Your body is your temple and paying attention to what you eat and how you sustain that body is self-respecting, self loving and necessary.

How to find the proper foods for you?

Make a list of what and how you eat throughout your week. Be honest: do you eat a proper breakfast, do you eat in a hurry, do you eat late in front of TV? How much dairy, bread, pasta, sugars, candies, cookies, junk food, ice cream, vegetables, fruits and freshly made foods do you consume? How much time do you take when selecting and preparing your food? What constitutes your usual breakfast? If your answer is that you are not hungry in the morning and a Starbucks coffee is all you require, think again.

I am always concerned when a client reveals a completely ignorant habit regarding what foods they consume. And on the other hand, I get also optimistic, because I know how much their health will improve just by beginning to eat healthy.

Your body is an amazing instrument that will eventually let you know if something does not agree with it. Your body has a high tolerance and will give you time, hoping that your bad eating habits are just temporary. The damaging effects will be absorbed into your system and your body will patiently wait for your attention, eventually giving you little signs that something is amiss. When you still do not pay attention to these signs, as a consequence - bigger signs will appear. Your body is making an effort to communicate and yet more often than not, even serious ailments will be ignored unless the situation develops into a critical state. An illness, a physical discomfort or pain will require your attention. Now the crisis is real, the wake up call can't be ignored. You are in a state of panic – "what did I do wrong, why me, why now - such bad timing". And yet all this time, you have not been listening, not paying attention, ignoring your body and living completely disconnected from it.

This does not speak only of your diet, but all aspects of your life. Everything combined: your actions, your diet, your emotions, your experiences and your physical body's limitations have brought you now here to this place where you are forced to listen, pay attention and do "something ". If you do not deal with the source of your problem, you could eventually find yourself in an even more challenging position. It is time to listen to your body, and become aware of your diet and your daily routine. There are also many who consume a healthy diet and still experience illness. In such a case, there are other lifestyle factors that have contributed to this unharmonious state, perhaps deeper emotional issues that need to be addressed. An unhappy relationship where you stay physically present, but are emotionally absent is very unhealthy and can be a source of great challenge for your entire body and mind.

A healthy diet will help sustain you and anchor your physical body in an optimal state so that you will be able to successfully overcome any other challenging issue with greater strength and positive outcome.

By now everyone knows that junk food is very damaging to your health. But it is not as simple as that. You need to know and understand your body to truly find the perfectly balanced diet that suits your specific needs. Observing basic rules of consuming fresh organic fruits and vegetables, staying away from sugar, eliminating gluten, selecting healthy fats and sources of protein - all those aspects take some effort and discipline. Whatever your individual physical needs are, you need to adjust your diet. Limit unhealthy foods as much as possible or completely and avoid dead foods - they have little or no live energy. You will experience positive results fairly quickly. Select foods that are vibrant, alive and can provide fresh live energy and positively affect your energy body as well.

I recommend a mostly alkaline foods diet as it helps your body to maintain an optimal state of health. A healthy balance is combined of 80% Alkaline foods and no more than 20% Acidic foods. Too much acidity in your body creates a thriving environment for illness and unbalance. Keeping your body as alkaline as possible will help you manage challenging situations with greater ease, but it will take some effort and discipline. Once you establish a healthy regimen, it will be much less appetizing to go back to the old unhealthy diet habits. You will feel a physical improvement of your overall state and no amount of temporary eating pleasure of sweets will be worth it to go back to the old ways.

One last tip: drink generous amounts of fresh clean water and add some fresh lemon - it creates an instant alkaline drink and is wonderful for flushing out your toxins. Prepare and eat your food with loving demeanor, with positive emotional disposition and in a peaceful calm environment, focusing only on enjoying every bite of nature's healthy nourishment.

ALKALINE VEGETABLES

ALKALINE FRUITS

ALKALINE FOODS THAT TASTE ACIDIC

ACIDIC FOODS

YOUR ENVIRONMENT

Your environment plays a major role in your overall energy, emotional, mental and physical state. Your environments are where you live, sleep, eat, work and play. Your home environment is most important. You may be able to tolerate a stressful job environment to a certain degree better, if your home is peaceful, loving and nurturing. But you can not expect to function at your optimal level, if your work environment is more peaceful than your home. If you find yourself escaping to your office, you are obviously not dealing with some serious issues at home. Home is where you must be able to rest, feel undisturbed, sleep peacefully and eat with awareness. It is truly of great importance to create that peaceful haven at home. If certain aspect are preventing you from being able to fulfill this essential need, you need to look at your life, acknowledge what is the challenging issue and embark on a change. If you keep ignoring or avoiding this problem, life will eventually force you into action, but often in a much more painful way. No matter what craziness surrounds you at work, by being able to completely regenerate at home, you will be able to withstand enormous challenges with ease. By assuring a place of rest where you can enjoy peaceful sleep, you will awaken prepared for anything.

Do whatever you can to create that temple at home, even if it just a small corner in a room where you can meditate and other family members know and respect your private space of peace, stillness and absolutely do not disturb you. If you are a busy parent, teach your children to respect your space or include them into short daily practice of stillness. If your baby is taking a nap, don't go crazy cleaning the house - take a break, meditate, breathe and replenish. Everything else can wait.

If you work from home, the situation requires a different dynamic. Separating work from home life demands clear boundaries for yourself and others. Create a pleasant and relaxing space in your home office, take regular breaks and make a point to have a different area in your home for complete relaxation. If you work on a computer, do not remain in your home office surfing the web endlessly – even while trying to relax. Change the environment - go outdoors, look at nature, sit in a park - do whatever it takes to provide some healing energy and recharging elements for your senses.

If your regular work environment is very stressful, find a small area where you can go during breaks to refresh, breathe, have a sip of water, and relax for a few minutes. Pace yourself, do not go on like a hectic express train. Do not overheat your inner engine.

When you feel the need to cleanse your home, use a sage smudge wand to clear the area. This is especially important if a negative event took place, an argument, depression or sad occasion. Open the windows and doors, make a draft and clear the space airing it out, allowing new clean energy to enter. Keep your time on computers limited, keep them out of your bedroom, or turn them off (or sleep mode) at night and when not in use. Always wear earphones when using cellular phone and turn it off while sleeping. Do not hold that powerful device so close to your sensitive brain! Be conscious of electromagnetic vibrations in your nearest vicinity. Make an effort to create an emotionally and mentally clear and clean home environment, free of electromagnetic pollution.

YOUR RELATIONSHIPS

The key to healthy relationships is your relationship with yourself. It sets a precedent for all other relationships.

All relationships in your life have a profound effect on you and your energy body. More often than not, these effects are not visible to your eye, but they certainly are there. If you are surrounded by supportive and happy people and enjoy healthy relationships, you will find a sense of strength and your inner balance will be magnified. But of course life is not usually just a happy ride where all relationships are wonderful and everything is rosy. Here we will address the dynamics of intimate relationships, because they have the most profound effect on your physical and energy body.

In an intimate relationship, the subtle energy exchange is extensive and long lasting. During a love relationship, invisible energy cords develop between the two partners and any disharmony greatly affects both partners and also transfers to the other partner. If a relationship is broken, these energy cords are torn which can often be experienced as actual physical pain. The energy cords are often the challenge, even when partners know it is in both of their best interest's to go their separate ways, for even a physical distance does not disconnect these cords immediately. It makes it also more difficult for one person to try to break free of a relationship, when the other partner has literally an energetic pull with the cord attached to them and can continuously pull them back. To an outsider it may seem like an unexplainable dynamic, why someone would not leave a bad and even abusive relationship, but it is often physically challenging because of these strong energetic connections that need to be severed. It takes time, strength and conscious separation. If the dynamic is unbalanced and one partner is energetically depleting the other, the chances for the weaker partner to leave the relationship become even more difficult. Harmony helps the separation move faster, conflict and unresolved issues delay the separation process by keeping the connecting energy cord alive with energy of negative emotions. Being aware of these subtle energy dynamics can be very helpful.

Learning obstacles are placed in your way from your birth till your last day on earth. Challenging set-up's with parental figures remain with us for decades no matter where we later physically reside in relation to them. Physical distance does not resolve the conflicting issues automatically. Dynamics that are complex affect our relationships with others, especially our intimate partners. Why? Because the first childhood "role models" which were our parents have perhaps established a challenging dynamic that we have been brought up with, recognizing it as our "normal". If one parent is absent, that is the "normal" for the child. If the parents are divorced, that is the "normal" for that child. If the parents are happily together, than this is the child's "normal". If the parents are unhappy, together living in complex dysfunctional, abusive and conflicting relationship, that is unfortunately still the "normal" for the child. It is what the child sees, experiences and lives with every day. A million versions can occur – all of them experienced as that particular child's "normal" life. The child and later grown individual will be inclined to build their life based on these dynamics and rules, their emotional receptivity and comfort with their future partners will most likely have some element of parental relationship dynamic they lived with as children. This will be a predisposition, but not necessarily the final result. They will have to overcome the obstacles and learn to establish new healthy dynamics. Yes, it makes everything supremely complex and intricate, but most importantly we are not addressing this issue to blame our parents for all the mishaps of our life. We are only being encouraged to recognize, explore and bring awareness to these dynamics, so that we may attempt to successfully resolve the greatest mystery of all - ourselves.

This is an essential step for healthy relationships; to be able to be as balanced as possible in order to hopefully attract an equally balanced partner into your energy field. Once established, the relationship has a life of its own – continuously changing, growing, sometimes closer and other times apart. If you remain with one partner for the duration of your life, you will experience countless changes like everyone else. Certainly those changes will differ from someone else's, who has lived thru many relationships and experienced various life partners. What are the consequences? Infinite possibilities exist, the key element is that you remain in a healthy emotional, mental and consequently best physical condition thru all these life changes and experiences.

You will get scars and you will experience thrills, it is all a part of life- making peace with it is your option. Healing wounds is important, being patient with the process takes time and clear intention.

It is important to be aware of damaging aspects of bad relationships that, if left ignored and continuously present, will consequentially negatively affect your health.

Unspoken words, bad communication, grudges, unresolved conflicts, blame, guilt, jealousy, hurt and pain, physical, emotional and mental abuse...these are the harmful dynamics of a relationship that are damaging to your health.

You may not be able to control the onset or prevent these challenging situations from happening, BUT you can decide how you will react to them and if, and how long, you will remain exposed to them.

It is your disposition towards unfortunate events that matters. If you communicate and express your feelings of hurt and pain inflicted, you will not carry them in your energy body in such toxic amounts.

If you and your partner manage to work thru bad dynamics, transform them and grow - good for you. If you can't work thru them, it is your decision to remove yourself from the toxic unhealthy relationship and preserve your health. I know this is often much easier said than done. Being true to yourself and honest with your behavior and actions –that is essential. Self love and self-respect can be your mantra. Taking responsibility for your actions or passive demeanor is part of growing process. If you do not choose to do that, you will stagnate, always blaming others for unfortunate circumstances and your misery.

A harmonious relationship, where there is mutual respect, unconditional love and support, trust, flexibility with changes that naturally occur thru years - that is a healthy productive and fulfilling partnership.

Often an element of codependence can develop here and that may be a challenge when one of you leaves this world before the other. Then you will have the opportunity and undoubtedly challenge, to practice and explore your independence and strength in a whole new way.

Life is a school, there is no better way to put it. Relationships are fantastic training ground. Whatever destiny holds for you, that is your path. If you are fortunate to have a life long partner, so be it. If your path is different and you find yourself often alone, accept this dynamic and learn to be happy with your own company.

This is actually a good prerequisite for a healthy functioning relationship anyway. Learning to be happy before meeting your love is a gift- the expectations and pressure for the loved one to be the answer and source for your happiness is transformed, and you both can enjoy the relationship on an equal level.

An unhappy intimate relationship can create seriously damaging health consequences. That is a fact. Decades - long unhappy state will manifest in a form of a physical ailment or illness.

For example; if a woman quietly suffers in an unhappy relationship where there is betrayal, grief, sadness and hurt, she will most likely develop problems in her breasts - her fourth chakra center will be oversaturated with unresolved dense negative energy. Keep in mind, this unhappiness can certainly come from another close emotional relationship that is hurtful and harmful to her, like a difficult child or parent etc.

If she is silently unhappy and emotionally absent during intercourse, she will suffer from reproductive system difficulties and health challenges. Any of these ailments will occur, if she is continuously and -for an extended period of time- energetically blocking her partner's physical contact. If she is not physically blocking the partner and passively participates -the damage to her energy body is even deeper. The energy exchange during intercourse is complex and her aversion will be agitated and magnified when it is ignored. Finally, her body will create and illness to help prevent the physical contact completely.

If there are numerous other forms of disharmony in relationship, where there is mental abuse or stress, health consequences will manifest.

When the unhappiness lies with the male partner as in abusive behavior, unharmonious sexual relationship, lack of, over activity, dishonesty, guilt and uncontrolled addiction, consequently health issues will develop within his physical body as well. One always has to explore all the elements that could be present in an intimate relationship and honestly assess the situation from all sides.

With open communication you can often overcome obstacles and improve dynamics. The worst case scenario is silent suffering or abuse. The best case scenario is open communication, honesty, trust, respect and love, and if separation is necessary and unavoidable, the courage and strength to do so.

SELF-LOVE

Love is everything. This may sound like a very general statement, but whatever your life's journey is, I can guarantee it is going to be much better with love in it. No need to wait for others to love you. You need to first know how to truly love yourself. Self-respect and self-love are necessary and essential for your overall healthy emotional, mental and physical state. If you love yourself in a healthy way, you set an example for others in how you should be treated, respected and ultimately loved. Your disposition towards yourself in your daily life is a direct expression of your love for yourself. Are you the last one in line of priorities? How do you expect to be able to take care of others if you do not care for yourself? Your love for yourself is expressed thru three basic areas: your kindness and care for you body, your emotional feelings about yourself and of your mental – inner dialogue with yourself.

How do you treat your body? Do you feed it properly, do you take care of any small discomfort or ailment, do you register and recognize a signal when something doesn't agree with it? Do you give it proper rest, fresh air, exercise and a healing environment? Paying attention to your physical self demonstrates your self-respect and self-love.

What about your feelings? Are you critical of your body's appearance, unhappy about your shape and proportions? Consciously express loving emotions instead and observe the improvement in your overall state.

Last but not least, your mind and your inner dialogue about your physical self is also very important. Take a moment and pay attention to this aspect. What are the words in your mind when you see your reflection, what kind of message are you sending yourself? Your environment can certainly influence you in this aspect as the society promotes massive pressure on a fashionable look, whatever that is. It is quite impossible to squeeze oneself into the parameters of what is generally considered beautiful. Every visual display in media promotes beauty that is practically computer generated. A much better solution is to create your own standards for your beautiful, healthy self. Size does not matter, what matters is your optimal healthy and vibrant energy state. Find your own individual healthy comfort zone where you are fulfilled in regards to your physique. A healthy person that pays attention to a happy emotional and mental disposition will always look beautiful with a magical glow that nothing else can compare to, shining brighter than you can imagine. How can you achieve that?

Love all aspects of yourself with intention and discipline. And faster than you can imagine, you will also attract love – it will come to you from everywhere.

YOUR HABITS AND ADDICITONS

An important part of a healthy lifestyle is exploring your daily habits and addictions. I say addictions with some hesitance because I know you will think: What, I am not an addict!!

But addiction comes in many shapes and colors. Yes, drugs, alcohol and smoking are the damaging addictions we are all too familiar with. No need to write how those addictions work and how complex the healing process can be. What I want to address here is other addicitons that get less attention, like addiction to food, sugar, addiction to certain activities like gambling, sex, shopping, extreme dieting and addiction to certain emotional states like drama, conflict, victimization, violence etc.

Activities like excessive work can be addictive as well. When all your life is and revolves only around work, you need to take a step back and reflect for a moment. Is this what your life is all about? What about other aspects? Are you just running away from loneliness, hurt, pain, fear…what is preventing you from finding inner balance?

Whatever you do, taking a healthy break and creating a harmony by including a variety of activities will make you a better person, partner, worker, and human being.

Addictions to certain kind of relationship dynamics are also unhealthy. Be present, see clearly what dysfunctional scenarios you continuously participate in, and acknowledge that you are addicted to the energy exchange that it demands. If you always argue, do you know how it is to not argue? Addiction to emotional states can also creep up on you before you know it. If you experience drama each and everyday, perhaps it is time to stop and honestly look if it is not you that has created all this drama – and why? Perhaps wanting the attention? Wanting sympathy, and some more attention. Or perhaps you simply don't know how it feels to be still, peaceful and quiet.

How about addiction to computers and internet? If you are constantly online - no matter how many times you run out of information to read, or cell phone – even if there is nothing seriously important to talk about – it sounds like you just feel the need to be busy and can't do without it.

How about the constant texting some people are addicted to? It is quite fascinating in a frightening way how cigarettes and fiddling with fingers and smoking has been replaced with cell phone texting. One bad addiction has been replaced with another. People seem to walk across the street without even making a slight effort to look at traffic- they are texting while walking! What could be so incredibly important that can not wait until you are still? And texting or talking on the phone while driving? It is ongoing and even if you wear earphones, why all the constant talking? It seems rare to find a person driving and concentrating exclusively on the road. The need for constant busyness, and mental distraction is frightening. It seems we have an incredibly hard time just walking the street alone- we don't know what to do with ourselves. We prefer not to look around and observe others or our environment, no, we prefer to stare at a tiny cell phone pad and pretend we are incredibly important and even more incredibly busy. People have an increasingly harder time practicing stillness and silence. Have you noticed how movies have gotten increasingly faster? The special effects are so crammed that it pains me how much time, work, effort, not to mention insane money is wasted for an effect that can't be even properly seen by the audience. Not to mention how violent and crazy the majority of the films have become. Are we addicted to violence, crazy noise, fast moving visuals and yet absolutely zero challenge for reflecting on the story, context, character development or the message, and is there even a message there? Or is it all just a non-stop sensory pounding overload that results in more numbness to violence and truly handicaps our delicate sensory organs. Of course not all films are that way, but sadly the majority of the ones for the mass- world audience are.

The point is that it would be beneficial for each and every one of us to occasionally stop and take a few moments to reflect on our everyday behavior, our usual emotional dynamics and make sure that we do not get into an unproductive addictive habit that will prove to have disturbing effects on our pursuit of a healthy lifestyle.

If you see yourself slipping into a habit of any kind, stop and honesty ask yourself why and do you really need to engage in, feel, or create this habit and what good will it bring you. Are you in charge of yourself or is your unhealthy habit taking the best of you? The only habit I can encourage you to do, is daily practice of stillness and leading a healthy lifestyle in every singular possible aspect.

TAKING RESPONSIBILITY FOR YOUR HEALING PROCESS

When facing a challenging health issue it is of most importance to establish an honest communication with yourself. Being aware of how you feel physically, emotionally and mentally plays a decisive role in your healing process. Why? Because it is a result of these factors that greatly contribute to the onset of an illness.

Even if your illness may be a result of outside factors, genetic predispositions or contagious circumstances, your body system usually has strong defensive options to help fight off an illness. But, if your body is weak and not in it's optimal state, it will have a challenging time defending itself. For example, if you are predisposed to an illness, a generally unhealthy lifestyle will prompt this illness to manifest in a much more aggressive and quicker way. If under the same predisposed circumstances you lead a healthy lifestyle, the illness will manifest in a weaker form or possibly not at all. If you have the misfortune of an unexpected accident, your body will recover much faster when healthy. Otherwise this accident will trigger a chain reaction of other deeper weaknesses within your physical system. The consequence can be the onset of a chronic illness. No matter what comes your way, your overall state of general health plays a decisive role when recovering and overcoming any health challenges.

By taking responsibility for keeping your body in it's optimal state of health, you have taken charge and effectively prevented or completely eliminated future possible health challenges.

If you are already dealing with a health issue, your full and committed attention is needed in your physical, mental and emotional bodies. By participating with awareness and intention thru the healing process, the positive results are magnified and will occur much faster.

PART 3.

HOW to PRACTICE
MUDRA THERAPY

WHERE CAN YOU PRACTICE MUDRAS

Daily Mudra practice will help you release old, draining, unhealthy energies and will recharge you with new and vibrant life force that is essential for your health. Mudras can be practiced anyplace and anytime you can find a few minutes to yourself. It is preferable to find a quiet and peaceful place where no one can disturb you. When you are new to Mudras it is important that you can fully experience the effects without distractions. Proper breathing is essential and should be practiced in a quiet environment so that you can hear yourself breathe. Once you have become familiar with the practice, you can practice the Mudras in any environment. Mudras should not be practiced on a full stomach, it is best to wait at least an hour after a big meal.

For best effects practice the Mudras first thing in the morning to begin your day and in the evening before retiring, for a restful and rejuvenating sleep. For an extended practice, wrap a shawl around your shoulders and body as you body temperature may drop slightly during Mudra and meditation practice.

When practicing Mudra Therapy for specific health ailment or challenging condition, it is best to establish a regular location in your home where you can practice completely undisturbed and in peace.

HOW OFTEN AND HOW LONG

For very specific selected therapeutic effects, your Mudra practice needs to be more engaging and longer than regular Mudra practice which requires as little as a minimum of three minutes for a Mudra.

In Mudra Therapy, your basic regular practice needs to be extended to 31 minutes. In that length of time, your inner stability is achieved, your energy body aura layers are integrated and begin to positively affect all of your body's complex elements and aspects.

You may extend your practice to 62 minutes for faster results. This provides ample time for your entire being to absorb and integrate this newly established positive energetic state and hold it for an extended period of time.

By providing more and longer opportunities for your body to experience these stimulating and revitalizing healing effects, you will help establish a new positive self- healing habit and will be able to permanently maintain the desired healthy state.

Final word; for optimal results practice Mudra Therapy every day for at least 31 minutes.

MUDRA THERAPY POSTURE

Sit in a comfortable position with a straight back and completely relax your shoulders and neck. Select the best seating option, on the floor, on a chair or on bed, wherever you can create comfort. If sitting on a chair, keep both feet equally on ground. Sitting is the best position, but if your health condition prevents you from sitting, you may practice Mudras while lying down.

Your eyes are an important part of your practice. They may remain half open and gently directed towards the tip of your nose or you may close your eyes and *gently* direct them toward the area of the Third Eye. If you prefer to keep your eyes open, relax the eyelids and direct your eyes into the middle distance. Never force your eyes into an uncomfortable or painful position.

After adjusting your posture and your eyes, place your hands in the Mudra position and begin with practice.

MUDRA THERAPY BREATH CONTROL

Proper breathing is essential for your Mudra practice. Inhale and exhale only through the nose unless otherwise specified. For most of the Mudras your breathing should be deep, slow, and calm, centered at the solar plexus area. Avoid lifting the shoulders and breathing from the upper chest area. When you inhale, your solar plexus should expand, and when you exhale, it should contract. Focusing your breath on the stomach area will help alleviate stress, fear, anger, and many other negative emotions you may hold there. With each deep inhalation and exhalation you are helping your body release toxins and bring in oxygen – a vital element for your optimal heath.

In addition to this deep, log breathing, Mudras sometimes require a technique called the breath of fire. It works under the same principles from the solar plexus area, but at a faster pace. In this case you place the emphasis on the exhalation and each breath lasts about a second. It is very important that you master the deep, log breathing first and then slowly increase the speed of your breathing to the breath of fire. When you're starting out, practice the breath of fire for a short time – no more than a minute - and then return to the deep, long breath. With time, increase the breath of fire with the corresponding Mudras to three minutes maximum.

Avoid practicing the breath of fire if you have heart problems, high blood pressure and women should avoid it during heavy days of their cycle. The breath of fire energizes and stimulates your body, whereas the deep, long breathing calms and relaxes you. Both breathing techniques clear your body of toxins, help you stay healthy and energized, and give you glowing radiant skin and clear eyes.

The following Mudras are excellent for learning proper breathing and feeling the correct expansion of chest with each breath, without lifting shoulders or straining.

MUDRA for Activating the Lower Chakras - page 105

MUDRA for Uplifting Your Heart - page 106

MUDRA for Energy in Upper Chakras - page 107

PROPER MUDRA HAND POSITIONS

It is essential that Mudras be practiced precisely as depicted and described. The position of each finger matters and hand levels and positions in relation to your body are most important. The same Mudra is not going to have equal effect when held lower - closer to your solar plexus or above your head. This detail matters much. Extend the fingers, hold the elbows nicely elevated as needed and concentrate on remaining in Mudra position for the duration of the entire practice. Do not lower your elbows, slouch or give up, but strive to complete each practice. With time, discipline and persistence, you will build up your stamina, gain much inner strength, confidence and experience a magnified power or body and mind.

CONCENTRATION

During Mudra Therapy practice you can use your concentration skills for a specific health improvement. The state of your mind and focused attention is of great importance. A positive, optimistic and determined state of mind is a decisive factor in your healing process. In each Mudra Therapy set you will find instructions for your concentration and focus.

MEDITATION

You may meditate before, during or after Mudra therapy. This is the time when you become still, free your mind, and expand your awareness beyond limitations. Meditation has many healing effects on your entire being. Clinical research has shown that regular meditation successfully and positively affects your capacity to concentrate, improves circulation, lowers blood pressure, releases stress, strengthens your nervous system, helps with depression, migraine headaches, insomnia, eliminates addictions, and improves your overall immune system. All these benefits are magnified and extended when combined with Mudra Therapy.

VISUALIZATION

Your mind has an energy body layer of it's own and it is an immensely powerful and important participant in your healing process. Visualization is like a rehearsal in your mind of something positive you desire to accomplish, experience or attract. A negative visualization can be detrimental to your health. A positive, strong and confident visualization of yourself in a healthy state is most effective and will play a decisive role in your recovery. When facing health challenges we are often overwhelmed with fear. That prompts frightening worst case scenarios in your mind, resulting in more distress. When dealing with a health challenge, you will considerably speed your recovery if you visualize yourself in a healthy and vibrant state, having overcome the ailment. During Mudra Therapy you are mentally in an ideal place to practice positive visualization. Combining these two modalities will increase positive healing effects.

AFFIRMATION AND PRAYER

Affirmations are a great technique to direct your mind power in the positive self - healing direction of your choice. The inaudible voice in your head, the inner monologue you conduct during the day, each and every word of it carries a specific mental frequency. It is of highest importance to pay attention to how you think and what you "hear" in your mind. During Mudra Therapy your mind is open and receptive to new information providing an excellent opportunity to consciously choose a positive affirmation for your successful healing process. Prayer has powerful positive effects and you may enrich your practice with a personal prayer that will maintain a steady support in your subconscious mind. You may practice and affirmation at least 5 minutes - 1 minute aloud, 1 minute whispering, 1 minute silently and back to 1 minute whispered and 1 minute spoken out loud affirmation.

MANTRA

The healing power of sound vibrations can be activated by singing mantras. The hard palate in your mouth has fifty-eight energy points that connect to and affect your entire being. By singing, speaking, or whispering mantras you are touching these energy points in a specific order and pattern that has a harmonizing and healing effect on your physical, mental and emotional energy body. The ancient science of mantras helps you activate and fine-tune your energy frequency to the optimal harmonious state.

The healing effect of the sound resonates with each chakra and energy body layer. By singing the basic mantra OOMMM you are resonating your charkas in order from first upwards to seventh. Take a deep breath and slowly sing A-E-I-O-U-M and feel the sound vibration travel thru your body upwards, ending in your forehead. Mantras practiced with Mudra Therapy magnify these ancient self-healing techniques and let you experience and benefit from multidimensional healing.

HOW TO BEGIN YOUR MUDRA THERAPY PROCESS

This guidebook will take you through step by step process to experience most benefits from a practice that is specified to your current needs.

This discipline is quite engaging and will help you explore yourself, find your shortcomings, discover your habits and consciously recreate a new healthy you.

In the following chapter you will find the long list of Mudras for various purposes and needs. Become familiar with them and if you are ready, you may begin your practice right away. Select Mudras that best suit your current needs. To help you easily establish that, you can compose an assessment chart that will clearly indicate in which areas you need help.

YOUR ASSESSMENT CHART

Before commencing, you need to establish a clear picture of your current emotional, mental and physical state. Get a piece of paper and compose your chart. You need to be clear in three areas of your current state.

PHYSICAL AWARENESS

In order to become fully present and aware of your physical body and it's current condition, you need to be calm, centered and bring awareness into your physical self. In your mind, scan your body from your feet upwards to the top of your head. Describe your general state and any smaller discomforts that burden you. Now your awareness is beginning to focus in order to be able to find relief and help re-establish a state of comfort and vitality to your physical self.

Example:
My body feels :
tired, depleted, back pain

Taking into account where your physical discomforts lie, have a clear picture of where you want and need to experience improvement.
Now clearly describe your optimal physical condition as if your problem is resolved. This is now your affirmation for your new reality you are creating.

Your new affirmation for your physical state:
My body feels refreshed, energized, healthy and pain free.

YOUR EMOTIONS
Often in can be quite daunting to openly admit to yourself that you feel sad, hurt or afraid. By writing it down, you are taking first step towards overcoming an unpleasant emotion you wish to eliminate. I suggest that you write down the first emotion that comes to your mind, it usually is the correct answer to describe your state.
Example:
My emotional state is sad, hurt, heartbroken

Now consciously take a step into the new direction. Clearly select how you want to feel - be free, generous and think big.
Affirm this new desired state as if it has been accomplished and achieved.

Your new affirmation for your emotional energy body:
I feel content, happy, my heart is healed

YOUR MENTAL STATE
This is the next state that needs your attention and recalibration. Write down your main mental disposition.
Example:
My thoughts are negative, pessimistic, self-scolding

Changing any element of this inner mental dialogue requires your clear mental picture of what you want to change and improve. You can redirect your mind pattern as you consciously decide. Now create your new chosen mental disposition that you intend to practice.

My new mental affirmation:
*My mind power is unlimited, I am creating a
fulfilled life and making progress as I envisioned.*

Now you have created a clear chart that will help you navigate through selecting appropriate Mudras that will help you eliminate and overcome your current challenging condition and are the perfect fit for your needs. To reaffirm the new desired positive state, select Mudras that strengthen those aspects.

In the following pages you will find 78 Mudras to select from, for your individual practice. Each Mudra has clearly described instructions for practice.
For more complex ailments refer to Chapter 5. You will find Mudra Therapy Sets that will guide you thru specific Mudra Therapy combinations and detailed sensory healing aspects to assure your optimal healing process.

There are four Mudras at the very end of Chapter 4. that are appropriate for personal prayer and can be added to the end of any sequence, depending on your personal preference. These are Mudra for Evoking the Sacred Scent of perfume, Mudra for Calling the Gods of Earth, Mudra for Evoking the Power of Jupiter and Mudra for Receiving God's law.

Enjoy the Mudra Practice and remember, disciplined regular practice will establish powerful and healthy new dynamics within your energy body. When Mudras become a part of your daily life, they will create the desired effects almost in an instant.

PART 4.

78 MUDRAS

Mudra for Developing Meditation

CHAKRA: All chakras
HEALING COLOR: All colors

Sit with a straight spine. With the four fingers of your right hand feel the pulse on your left wrist. Press lightly and feel the pulse in each fingertip.
Close your eyes and concentrate on your Third ye.
With each beat of your pulse, mentally repeat the mantra.
BREATH: Long, deep and strong
MANTRA: *SAT NAM*
(Truth Is God's Name, One in Spirit)

Mudra for Divine Worship

CHAKRA: All chakras
HEALING COLOR: All colors

Sit with a straight spine. Place your palms together in front of your chest.
Sit still and concentrate on your Third Eye for at least three minutes.
BREATH: Long, deep and strong
MANTRA: *EK ONG KAR*
(One Creator, God Is One)

Mudra for Universal Energy and Eternity

CHAKRA: Base of spine - 1, Crown - 7
HEALING COLOR: Red, violet

Sit with a straight spine and bend your elbows, bringing your hands up
and away from your body so as to form two V's. Raise your palms
to just below your heart level, with fingers close together.
Be still and feel the energy flowing into your hands.
BREATH: Long, deep and strong
MANTRA: *HAR HARE HAREE WAHE GURU*
(God, the Creator of Supreme Power and Wisdom,
the Spiritual Teacher and Guide Through Darkness)

Mudra for Overcoming Anxiety

CHAKRA: Heart 4, Throat 5, Third Eye 6
HEALING COLOR: Green, blue, indigo

Sit with a straight back. Bend your elbows and raise your arms so your upper arms are parallel to the ground and extended out to the sides. Your hands are at the level of your ears, fingers spread wide and pointing up to the sky. Start rotating your hands back and forth, pivoting at the wrists. Practice for three minutes and be persistent. You will go thru a period that seems difficult, but when you overcome that moment, the practice will become easy. Relax, rest, and enjoy the stillness.
BREATH: Long, deep and strong
MANTRA: *HARKANAM SAT NAM*
(God's Name Is Truth)

Mudra for Preventing Burnout

CHAKRA: Base of the Spine 1, Reproductive organs 2, Solar plexus 3
HEALING COLOR: Red, orange, yellow

Sit with a straight spine. Bring your forearms up in front of you at heart level and bend your elbows to the side. With the palms facing the ground, fold your thumbs across the palm of each hand till they reach the bases of your ring fingers. Now bend your fingers slightly and touch the backs of your fingertips together, forming a V-shape with your hands. Hold for three minutes. Making sure your elbows remain elevated. Relax and rest.
BREATH: Long, deep and strong
MANTRA: *OM*
(God in His Absolute State)

Mudra for Recharging

CHAKRA: Base of the Spine 1, Reproductive organs 2, Crown 7
HEALING COLOR: Red, orange, violet

Sit with a straight spine. Extend your arms in front of you, parallel to the ground, keeping your elbows straight. Make a fist with your right hand and wrap the left hand around the right wrist. The bases of the palms are touching and the thumbs are straight up.
BREATH: Long, deep and strong

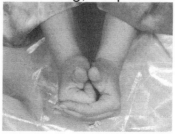

Mudra for Preventing Stress

CHAKRA: Solar plexus 3
HEALING COLOR: Yellow

Sit with a straight back. Bend your elbows and bring your forearms in front
of your solar plexus area parallel to the ground. Rest the back of the left
hand in the palm of the right hand, both palms facing up.
Fingers are straight and together.
Hold for three minutes and concentrate on your breath
BREATH: Long, deep and strong

Mudra for Help with a Grave Situation

CHAKRA: Heart 4
HEALING COLOR: Green

Sit with a straight spine. Bend your elbows and place both palms on your
upper chest, fingers pointing toward each other.
Hold and feel the healing energy of your hands soothe the heart.
BREATH: Long, deep and strong
MANTRA: *HUMME HUM, BRAHAM HUM, BRAHAM HUM*
(Calling upon Your Infinite Self)

Mudra for Protecting Your Health

CHAKRA: All chakras
HEALING COLOR: All colors

Sit with a straight back. Bend your right elbow and lift your hand up, palm facing out. The index and middle fingers are pointing up; the rest are curled with the thumb over. Hold your left hand in the same Mudra with the two stretched fingers touching your heart. Hold for three minutes.
BREATH: Inhale for ten counts, hold the breath for ten counts, and exhale for ten counts
MANTRA: *OM*
(God in His Absolute State)

Mudra for Strong Nerves

CHAKRA: Solar plexus 3, Heart 4
HEALING COLOR: Yellow, green

Sit with a straight spine. Lift your left hand to ear level, palm facing out. Connect the thumb and middle finger and stretch out the other fingers. Place your right hand in front of the solar plexus, palm facing up. The thumb and little fingers are touching while the other fingers are straight. **This position is reversed for men.**
BREATH: Inhale in four counts and exhale in one strong breath.

Mudra for Anti-aging

CHAKRA: Base of the spine 1, Reproductive organs 2
HEALING COLOR: Red, orange

Sit with a straight back and make circles with your thumbs and index
fingers. Stretch out the other fingers and
place your hands on your knees, palms facing up.
BREATH: Short, fast breath of fire, focusing on the navel
MANTRA: *EK ONG KAR SA TA NA MA*
(One Creator of Infinity, Birth, Death, and Rebirth)

Mudra for Sexual Balance

CHAKRA: Reproductive organs 2
HEALING COLOR: Orange

Sit with a straight back. With your elbows slightly to the sides, clasp your hands together. The fingers are intertwined. The right thumb on top of the left will empower the male side of your nature and the left thumb on top empowers the feminine, emotional side of your nature.
BREATH: Long, deep and strong

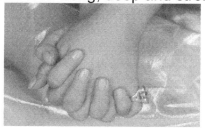

Mudra for Help with a Diet

CHAKRA: Base of spine 1, Solar plexus 3, Crown 7
HEALING COLOR: Red, yellow, violet

Sit with a straight back and extend your arms in front of you
parallel to the ground, palms facing up, slightly cupped. Inhale and move
your hands to the sides, as you exhale, return your hands to their original
position in front of you, but with your palms facing each other. Keep the
palms apart and be aware of the life force
that is being magnified between your hands. Repeat.
BREATH: Long, deep inhalation as you expand the arms, and exhalation
as you return them in front of you

Mudra for Facing Fear

CHAKRA: Solar plexus 3, Crown 7
HEALING COLOR: Yellow, violet

Sit with a straight spine. Bend your right elbow and lift the arm up to the level of your face. Face your palm outward, as if taking a vow. Bring your left arm in front of your navel, palm facing up. Concentrate on energy being received into your palms and hold for at least three minutes.
BREATH: Long, deep and slow.
MANTRA: *NIRBHAO NIRVAIR AKAAL MORT*
(Fearless, Without Enemy, Immortal Personified God)

Mudra for Trust

CHAKRA: Crown 7
HEALING COLOR: Violet

Sit with a straight spine. Make a circle with you arms arched up and over your head. Place the right palm on top of the left. Press the thumb tips together and visualize a protective circle of white light that surrounds you.
Men - put the left palm on top of the right.
BREATH: Short, fast breath of fire from navel
MANTRA: *HAR HAR HAR WAHE GURU*
(God's Creation, His Supreme Power and Wisdom)

Mudra for Love

CHAKRA: Heart 6
HEALING COLOR: Green

Sit with a straight spine and raise your hands to either side of your head.
Curl the middle and ring fingers into your palms and extend the thumbs,
index fingers, and little fingers. Keep your elbows from sinking
as you hold for three minutes.
BREATH: Inhale eight short counts, with one strong, long exhale
MANTRA: *SAT NAM WAHE GURU*
(God Is Truth, His Is the Supreme Power and Wisdom)

Mudra for Guidance

CHAKRA: Crown 7
HEALING COLOR: Violet

Sit with a straight spine. Bring your hands together at chest level as if forming a cup. The palms are facing up and the sides of the little fingers are pressed together. Focus your eyes past the tip of your nose toward your hands. Be still, hold and concentrate on your breath.
BREATH: Long, slow, and deep breath into the palms of your hands.
MANTRA: *SAT NAM*
(Truth Is God's Name, One in Spirit)

Mudra for Concentration

CHAKRA: Solar plexus 3, Heart 4, Crown 7
HEALING COLOR: Yellow, green, violet

Sit with a straight spine. Bend your elbows and bring your arms to your chest. Each thumb and index finger should form a circle. The index finger is curled far into the beginning of the thumb. The other fingers are stretched up. Connect your hands and outstretched fingers back to back. Be still, concentrate on your Third Eye.
BREATH: Long, deep and slow.
MANTRA: *AKAL AKAL AKAL HARI AKAL*
(Immortal Creator)

Mudra for Wisdom

CHAKRA: Solar plexus 3, Heart 4, Crown 7
HEALING COLOR: Yellow, green, violet

Sit with a straight spine and bend your elbows to the side, parallel to the ground. Make gentle fists, with the thumbs inside and the index fingers out. Now hook your index fingers around each other. The right palm is facing down and the left toward your chest.
BREATH: Long, deep and slow.
MANTRA: *SAT NAM*
(Truth Is God's Name, One in Spirit)

Mudra for Prosperity

CHAKRA: Base of spine 1, Reproductive organs 2, Solar plexus 3
HEALING COLOR: Red, orange, yellow

Sit with a straight spine. Bring your hands in front of you, fingers together and palms facing down. Press the sides of the index fingers together and hold for a second. Now turn your hands over so that the palms are facing up toward the sky for a second and the edges of the little fingers are touching. Keep repeating and chant the mantra HAR with each change of hand position. Continue the practice for eleven minutes and rest.
BREATH: Short, fast breath of fire from the point of the navel, repeated with each mantra and fast Mudra movement.
MANTRA: *HAR HAR*
(God, God)

Mudra for Stronger Character

CHAKRA: Solar plexus 3, Third Eye 6
HEALING COLOR: Yellow, indigo

Sit with a straight spine, hold your hands in relaxed fists at your sides.
Thumbs are on the outside and index fingers are straight and pointing up.
Lift your left hand to chin level and your right hand slightly higher, palms
facing each other. Hold, keeping your eyes open and looking forward.
BREATH: Long, deep and slow.
MANTRA: *HUMME HUM BRAHAM*
(Calling on the Infinite Self)

Mudra for Inner Integrity

CHAKRA: Throat 5, Third Eye 6
HEALING COLOR: Blue, indigo

Sit with a straight back. Bend your elbows and lift your upper arms parallel to the ground. Bring your hands to ear level, palms facing out. Curl your fingers inward and point the thumbs out toward your ears.
Hold for three minutes and relax.
BREATH: Short, fast breath of fire from navel.
MANTRA: *SAT NAM*
(Truth Is God's Name, One in Spirit)

91

Mudra for Taking Away Hardships

CHAKRA: Third Eye 6, Crown 7
HEALING COLOR: Indigo, violet

Sit with a straight spine and make fists with both hands, keeping the thumbs on the outside. Now swing your arms in big circles, like a pendulum. Begin with a movement forward and up, then go back and down. Repeat for three minutes.
BREATH: Long, deep and slow.
MANTRA: *HAR HARE GOBINDAY, HAR HARE MUKUNDAY*
(He Is My Sustainer, He Is My Liberator)

92

Mudra for Self - Confidence

CHAKRA: Solar plexus 3, Third Eye 6
HEALING COLOR: Yellow, indigo

Sit with a straight spine. Lift your hands up to the level of your solar plexus with elbows bent to the sides. Bend the middle, ring, and little fingers and touch them back to back. Extend the index fingers and thumbs and press them together. The thumbs are pointed toward you and the index fingers away from you. **BREATH**: Long, deep and slow.
MANTRA: *EK ONG KAR SAT GURU PRASAD,*
SAT GURU PRASAD EK ONG KAR (The Creator Is the One That Dispels Darkness and Illuminates Us by His Grace)

Mudra for Happiness

CHAKRA: Heart 4
HEALING COLOR: Green

Sit with a straight spine. Bend your elbows and bring your arms to your sides, away from your body. Elbows are just below the level of the shoulders. Palms are facing forward. Stretch the index and middle fingers and bend the ring and little fingers, pressing them into the palms firmly with the thumbs. Hold for three minutes and relax.
BREATH: Long, deep and slow.
MANTRA: *SAT NAM*
(Truth Is God's Name, one in Spirit)

94

Mudra for Contentment

CHAKRA: Solar plexus 3
HEALING COLOR: Yellow

Sit with a straight back and lift your hands in front of your stomach area.
Connect the thumb and the middle finger of the right hand and the thumb
and the little finger of the left hand. Relax the rest of the fingers and hold
your hands a few inches apart, palms up. Hold for three minutes, then
make fists with both hands and relax. **Men should practice the same
position with opposite hands. BREATH**: Long, deep and slow.
MANTRA: *SARE SA SA SARE SA SA SARE HARE HAR*
(God is Infinite in His Creativity)

Mudra for Tranquilizing the Mind

CHAKRA: Solar plexus 3, Heart 4, Throat 5, Third Eye 6
HEALING COLOR: Yellow, green, blue, indigo

Sit with a straight spine. Bend your elbows and bring your hands up to
your chest. Connect the middle fingertips and stretch them outward. Bend
the rest of the fingers and press them together along the second joint.
Connect your thumb tips and extend them toward you.
BREATH: Long, deep and slow.
MANTRA: *MAN HAR TAN HAR GURU HAR* (Mind with God, Soul with
God, the Divine Guide and His Supreme Wisdom)

96

Mudra for Diminishing Worries

CHAKRA: Heart 4, Throat 5, Third Eye 6
HEALING COLOR: Green, blue, indigo

Sit with a straight spine. Bring your hands in front of your chest with the palms facing up. The sides of the little fingers and the inner sides of the palms are touching. Now bring your middle fingertips together, perpendicular to the palms. Extend the thumbs away from the palms. Hold and keep the fingers stretched as little antennas for energy.
BREATH: Long, deep and slow.

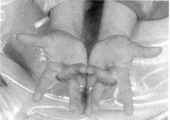

97

Mudra for Patience

CHAKRA: Third Eye 6, Crown 7
HEALING COLOR: Indigo, violet

Sit with a straight spine. Connect the fingertips of the thumbs and middle fingers, creating a circle. The rest of the fingers are outstretched. Lift your arms up at your sides so that your hands are at the level of your ears, palms facing outward. Keep your elbows nice and high for three minutes.
BREATH: Long, deep and slow.
MANTRA: *EK ONG KAR SAT GURU PRASAAD*
(One Creator, Illuminated by God's Grace)

Mudra for Inner Security

CHAKRA: Solar plexus 3, Heart 4
HEALING COLOR: Yellow, green

Sit with a straight spine and place your hands in reversed prayer pose:
hands touching back to back at the level of your heart and solar plexus.
Hold the pose for a beat, then repeat with palms pressed together in a
prayer pose, thumbs against the chest. Hold for a beat and repeat.
BREATH: Long, deep and slow.
MANTRA: *AD SHAKTI AD SHAKTI*
(I Bow to the Creator's Power)

Mudra for Higher Consciousness

CHAKRA: Solar plexus 3, Crown 7
HEALING COLOR: Yellow, violet

Sit with a straight back and lift your hands to solar plexus level with your palms together, fingers pointed away from you. Tuck your thumbs under so that their tips rest on the fleshy mounds below the little fingers. The bottoms of your hands touch firmly and your elbows are to either side.
BREATH: Long, deep and slow.

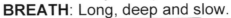

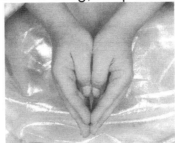

Mudra for Calming Your Mind

CHAKRA: Solar plexus 3, Crown 7
HEALING COLOR: Yellow, violet

Sit with a straight spine. Cross your arms in front of your chest, elbows bent at a ninety-degree angle and arms parallel to the ground. The right hand is on top of the left arm and left hand below the right arm. All fingers are together and straight. Hold and keep the arms from sinking for three minutes, then relax and be still.
BREATH: Long, deep and slow.
MANTRA: *OM*
(God in his Absolute State)

Mudra for the Lower Spine

CHAKRA: Base of spine 1, Reproductive Organs 2
HEALING COLOR: Red, Orange

Sit with a straight back and make fists with both hands. Leave the thumbs stretched out and place hands on your knees. The palms are facing the ground and the thumbs are directed towards each other. Keep the fists strong and feel the energy pulsating in your palms.
BREATH: Long, deep and strong
MANTRA: *OM*
(God in His Absolute State)

Mudra for the Middle Spine

CHAKRA: Solar Plexus 3, Heart 4
HEALING COLOR: Yellow, Green

Sit with a straight back and place your fists on your knees. Leave the
thumbs pointing up. Concentrate on your thumbs, sending healing energy
to the middle area of your back. Keep the thumbs stretched
and hold for three minutes.
BREATH: Long, deep and strong
MANTRA: *OM*
(God in His Absolute State)

Mudra for the Upper Spine Centers

CHAKRA: Throat 5, Third Eye 6, Crown 7
HEALING COLOR: Blue, indigo, violet

Sit with a straight back and place your fists on your knees palms up. Curl your fingers into fists, except for the thumbs, which are stretched out and pointed away from you, parallel to the ground. Concentrate on recharging and feel the energy in your thumbs activate your higher centers.
Hold for three minutes and relax.
BREATH: Long, deep and strong
MANTRA: *SAT NAM*
(Truth Is God's Name, One in Spirit)

Mudra for Activating the Lower Chakras

CHAKRA: Base of the spine 1, reproductive organs 2
HEALING COLOR: Red, orange

Sit with a straight back. Place both hands at waist level, thumbs open with palms facing down. All fingers are stretched and together, the tips of the middle fingers an inch apart. As you inhale, concentrate on expanding the lower area of your stomach. When you exhale, contract the stomach and bring your fingertips closer until they almost touch. Concentrate on bringing vital creative life force energy into that area.
BREATH: Start slowly and after a minute increase your breathing into the breath of fire. After a minute, slow down and return to the slow, deep breath.
MANTRA: *SAT NAM*
(Truth Is God's Name, One in Spirit)

105

Mudra for Uplifting Your Heart

CHAKRA: Heart 4,
HEALING COLOR: Green

Sit with a straight back and lift your arms up to shoulder level, elbows bent and parallel to the ground. Tuck your thumbs under your armpits and keep the rest of your fingers straight and together. Your hands should be above your breasts, palms facing down. As you inhale, the distance between middle fingertips gets bigger; as you exhale, the middle fingertips should touch or cross over each other. With each inhalation feel the healing energy expand your heart and chest area.
BREATH: Long, deep and slow

Mudra for Energy in Upper Chakras

CHAKRA: Throat 5, Third Eye 6, Crown 7
HEALING COLOR: Blue, indigo, violet

Sit with a straight back and place your hands above your head, palms pressed together, elbows to the side. Inhale and raise your hands as if someone were pulling them up. Exhale and lower your hands to a few inches above your head, palms always pressed together.
Repeat for three minutes.
BREATH: Inhale slowly when lifting hands,
and exhale deeply when lowering hands.
MANTRA: *SAT NAM*
(Truth Is God's Name, One in Spirit)

Mudra for Chakra I.& II.
Vitality and Letting Go

CHAKRA: Base of spine 1, Reproductive organs 2
HEALING COLOR: Red, orange

Sit with a straight back and place your fists on your knees, palms facing
up. Concentrate on your base chakra. Sit tall and attempt to stretch as if
trying to get taller. Be aware of the ground underneath you
and the life force of the earth.
BREATH: Long, deep and slow
MANTRA: *SAT NAM*
(Truth Is God's Name, One in Spirit)

Mudra for Chakra II.

CHAKRA: Reproductive organs 2
HEALING COLOR: Orange

Sit with a straight spine and bring your hands up to just below the throat. Cup your hands with palms up. The pinkies and thumbs are outstretched while the other three fingers are held together. The sides of little fingers are touching, and the thumbs are separated and pointing toward your body. Hold for three minutes.
BREATH: Long, deep and slow
MANTRA: *SAT NAM*
(Truth Is God's Name, One in Spirit)

Mudra for Chakra III.

CHAKRA: Solar plexus 3
HEALING COLOR: Yellow

Sit with a straight back. Bend your elbows and lift your hands up, elbows parallel to the ground. The palms are facing forward, all fingers together, except for the thumbs, which are pointing toward the ears. Hold and keep the elbows nice and high for three minutes.
BREATH: Short, fast breath of fire from the navel.
MANTRA: *SAT NAM*
(Truth Is God's Name, One in Spirit)

Mudra for Healing Your Heart Chakra IV.

CHAKRA: Heart 4
HEALING COLOR: Green

Sit with a straight back. Lift your right hand up, elbow bent, your hand at the level of your face. Make a fist and leave only the index finger extended, pointing up. Place your left hand to your chest above your breast, elbow parallel to the ground. Hold and feel the energy shifting in your body. Keep the elbows nice and high.
BREATH: Long, deep and slow.

Mudra for HealingYour Voice-Chakra V.

CHAKRA: Throat 5
HEALING COLOR: Blue

Sit with a straight back and bend your elbows, lifting them up parallel to the ground. Make fists with both hands, leaving the index fingers pointing straight up. Bring your hands up to either side of your head, palm facing you. Hold and be aware of the energy shift in your fingers.
BREATH: Long, deep and slow
MANTRA: *EK ONG KAR*
(One Creator, God Is One)

Mudra for Knowing Truth - Chakra VI.

CHAKRA: Third Eye 6
HEALING COLOR: Indigo

Sit with a straight back. Bend your elbows and lift your arms up to so that the elbows are parallel to the ground. Palms are facing out and all fingers are together. Hold for three minutes and concentrate on your Third Eye.
BREATH: Long, deep and slow
MANTRA: *EK ONG KAR*
(One Creator, God Is One)

Mudra for Opening Your Crown - Chakra VII.

CHAKRA: Crown 7
HEALING COLOR: Violet

Sit with a straight back and interlock your fingers, but keep the thumbs extended upward. Now bring your hands above your head so that your thumbs are pointed to the back. Hold for a minute and a half and feel the energy pulse in your thumbs as you keep them extended. Then lower your hands and bring them in front of your heart for minute and a half.
BREATH: Long, deep and slow

Mudra for Emotional Balance

CHAKRA: All
HEALING COLOR: All

Before this practice, drink a glass of water to balance the water in your system. Sit with a straight spine and place your hands with palms open under your armpits. Close your eyes, give yourself a hug, inhale and lift your shoulders toward your ears for a few moments; then exhale, lower your shoulders and relax. Repeat for three minutes.
BREATH: Long, deep and slow and observe your emotions calming down.
MANTRA: *SAT NAM*
(Truth Is God's Name, one In Spirit)

Mudra for Mental Balance

CHAKRA: All
HEALING COLOR: All

Sit with a straight spine and place your hands at solar plexus level in front of you and interlace the fingers backward with palms facing up. Fingers are pointing up and the thumbs are straight.
BREATH: Long, deep and slow
MANTRA: *GOBINDAY, MUKUNDAY, UDARAAY, APAARAY, HARYING, KARYNG, NIRNAMAY, AKAMAY*
(Sustainer, Liberator, Enlightener, Infinite, Destroyer, Creator, Nameless, Desireless)

Mudra for Releasing Negative Emotions

CHAKRA: Heart 4
HEALING COLOR: Green

Sit with a straight spine. Bend your arms and make fists with both hands.
Bring them up in front of your heart, left over right.
Cross the wrists over each other.
BREATH: Long, deep and slow

Mudra for Powerful Energy

CHAKRA: Heart 4, Throat 5, Third Eye 6
HEALING COLOR: Green, blue, indigo

Sit with a straight spine. Lift your hands in front of you at the solar plexus.
Place your ring fingers flat and straight together and interlace all other
fingers, the right thumb on top of the left.
BREATH: Long, deep and slow
MANTRA: *OOOOONG*
(God as a Creator in Manifestation)

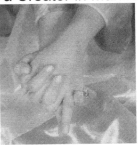

Mudra for Self - Healing

CHAKRA: Heart 4, Throat 5, Third Eye 6
HEALING COLOR: Green, blue, indigo

Sit with a straight back. Bring your arms up in front of your throat, fingers spread and outstretched. Connect the thumbs along their length and connect the tips of the pinkies. Bring your hands close to your nose.
BREATH: Inhale deeply and slowly through the nose and then close off the nostrils by placing the thumb tips over them. Hold the breath for as long as you can. Release the thumbs slightly to open the nostrils and exhale. Again hold the breath for as long as you possible before inhaling. Repeat the practice for three minutes.

Mudra for Preventing Exhaustion

CHAKRA: Solar plexus 3, Heart 4
HEALING COLOR: Yellow, green

Sit with a straight back. Lift your arms and grasp your earlobes with your thumbs and index fingers. Hold on to your ears and let the weight of your hands pull on them. Relax and feel the energy shifting in your head and body. Hold for three minutes and relax
BREATH: Long, deep and slow
MANTRA: *SAT NAM*
(Truth Is God's Name, One in Spirit)

Mudra for Rejuvenation

CHAKRA: Throat 5, Third eye 6, Crown 7
HEALING COLOR: Blue, indigo, violet

Sit with a straight back. Place both palms directly on your ears. Massage your ears in a circular motion away from your face – counter clockwise. Listen to the sound of "the ocean" you create with the palms of your hands and continue for at least three minutes.
BREATH: Long, deep and slow
MANTRA: *OM*
(God in His Absolute State)

Mudra for Strength

CHAKRA: Solar plexus 3, Heart 4
HEALING COLOR: Yellow, green

Sit with a straight back. Lift your hands up to the level of the heart and place your palms together. Fingers are spread apart. The thumbs are almost touching and the index and middle fingers are barely touching. Apply maximum force to the ring and little fingers. Concentrate on various pressures of our fingers, after three minutes relax, stretch arms above your head, then let down easy and rest.
BREATH: Very long, deep and slow
MANTRA: *SAT NAM*
(Truth Is God's Name, One in Spirit)

Mudra for Relaxation and Joy

CHAKRA: Solar plexus 3, Heart 4
HEALING COLOR: Yellow, green

Sit with a straight back and lift your hands up in front of your chest. Make a fist with your left hand, tucking the thumb inside. Wrap your right hand around the left and place your right thumb over the base of the left thumb. Concentrate on your Third eye area and hold for three minutes.
BREATH: Long, deep and slow
MANTRA: *HAREE HAR HAREE HAR*
(God in His Creative Aspect)

Mudra for Reproductive Center

CHAKRA: Reproductive organs 2
HEALING COLOR: Orange

Sit with a straight spine. Place your left hand with palm facing down in front of your stomach area. Hold your right hand open, away from your body, the palm facing up.
BREATH: Long, deep and slow
MANTRA: *SAT NAM*
(Truth Is God's Name, One in Spirit)

Mudra for Creativity

CHAKRA: Third Eye 6, Crown 7
HEALING COLOR: Indigo, violet

Sit with a straight spine. Connect the thumbs and index fingers, keeping the rest of the fingers straight. Bend your elbows and lift your hands to your sides with palms facing up at a sixty-degree angle to your body. Concentrate on your Third Eye center and meditate for at least three minutes.
BREATH: Short, fast breath or fire from the navel.
MANTRA: *GA DA*
(God)

Mudra for Opening Your Heart Center

CHAKRA: Heart 4
HEALING COLOR: Green

Sit with a straight spine. Lift your hands up in front of your heart and create a cup, palms facing each other, all fingers spread and pointing up. The upper parts of your thumbs and pinkies and the bases of your palms are touching. Visualize opening your heart, keeping fingers outstretched.
BREATH: Long, deep and slow.
MANTRA: *SAT NAM*
(Truth Is God's Name, One in Spirit)

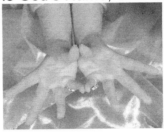

126

MUDRA THERAPY by Sabrina Mesko

Mudra of Open Heart

CHAKRA: Heart 4
HEALING COLOR: Green

Sit with a straight spine. Bend your elbows and lift your hands up in front
of your chest. The palms are looking up toward the sky and all fingers are
spread apart. The hands are not touching. Keep the fingers stretched out
as antennas of energy. Visualize your open heart
filled with glowing healing green or rose pink light.
BREATH: Long, deep and slow.

Mudra of Two Hearts

CHAKRA: Heart 4
HEALING COLOR: Green

Sit with a straight spine. Connect the thumbs and index fingers, forming a circle. Extend all other fingers, keeping them spread out. Lift your arms up in front of your heart, left over right, palms facing outward, and cross your wrists over each other. Hook your pinkies together, keep all fingers extended, hold for three minutes,
BREATH: Long, deep and slow.
MANTRA: *SAT NAM*
(Truth Is God's Name, One in Spirit)

Mudra for Empowering Your Voice

CHAKRA: Throat 5
HEALING COLOR: Blue

Sit with a straight back. Bend your elbows and hold them parallel to the ground as you bring your hands up in front of you at the level of your throat. Turn the right palm outward and the left palm toward you. Now bend your fingers and hook your hands together, the left hand on the outside. Pull on the hands as if trying to pull them apart, shoulders down.
BREATH: Long, deep and slow.

129

Mudra for Better Communication

CHAKRA: Base of the spine 1, Reproductive organs 2
HEALING COLOR: Red, orange

Sit with a straight spine. Connect the index finger and the thumb, creating a circle. Stretch out the rest of the fingers and rest your hands, palms facing down, on your thighs. Hold for three minutes, breathe and relax.
BREATH: Long, deep and slow.
MANTRA: *RAA MAA*
(I Am in Balance Between the Sun and the Moon, the Earth and the Ether)

Mudra for Finding the Perfect Truth

CHAKRA: Heart 4, Throat 5, Third Eye 6, Crown 7
HEALING COLOR: Green, blue, indigo, violet

Sit with a straight spine. Rest both hands on your knees, palms facing up toward the sky. Fingers are together and palms are very lightly cupped. Concentrate on your Third eye and enjoy stillness and peace.
BREATH: Long, deep and slow.
MANTRA: *SAT NAM*
(Truth Is God's Name, One In Spirit)

Mudra for Meditation of Change

CHAKRA: Third Eye 6, Crown 7
HEALING COLOR: Indigo, violet

Sit with a straight spine. Fold your fingers into fists, the fingertips pressing the upper pads of the hands. Press the backs of your hands together at the knuckles. The thumbs are extended and touching at the fingertips. Hold your hands in front of your navel with the thumbs directed slightly upward toward your heart. **BREATH**: Long, deep and slow.
MANTRA: *ONG NAMO GURU DEV NAMO*
(I Bow to the Infinity of the Creator, I call on the Infinite Creative Consciousness and Divine Wisdom)

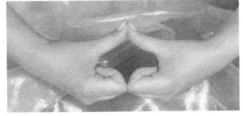

Mudra for Healthy Eyes

CHAKRA: Third Eye 6
HEALING COLOR: Indigo

Sit with a straight spine. Bring your arms up, at your sides, the palms turned in toward you. Now bring your palms together in front of your face, as if drawing a curtain. Open your arms, inhale, and look into the distance. Exhale when bringing your hands in font of your eyes and readjust the focus and look into your palms. This Mudra should be practiced every two hours for three minutes when working at a computer.
BREATH: Long, deep and slow.
MANTRA: *OM*
(God in his Absolute State)

Mudra for Brain Synchrony - Readjusting Your Perception

CHAKRA: Third Eye 6, Crown 7
HEALING COLOR: Indigo, violet

Sit with a straight spine. Make circles with the thumb and index fingers and spread out the rest of the fingers. Lift your arms so your elbows are perpendicular to the ground, hands eye level. Now move your hands toward each other until you can look through the openings in your fingers. As you separate your hands, take a long, slow inhale. As you bring them together in front of your face, exhale long, deep and slow. Repeat.
BREATH: Long, deep with hand movements.
MANTRA: *SA TA NA MA*
(Infinity, Birth, Death, Rebirth)

134

Mudra for Activating the Third Eye

CHAKRA: Third Eye 6
HEALING COLOR: Indigo

Sit with a straight spine. Connect the thumb and index fingers and extend
the rest of the fingers. Place your hands on your knees, palms facing up.
Concentrate on your third Eye and sit in complete stillness.
BREATH: Long, deep and slow.
MANTRA: *OM*
(God in His Absolute State)

135

Mudra for Taking You Out of Danger

CHAKRA: All Chakras
HEALING COLOR: All Color

Sit with a straight spine and raise your arms so that your hands are on either side of your face. Curl your fingers into fists, except for the thumbs, which should point gently toward the sky.
Continue holding for at least three minutes.
BREATH: Long, deep and slow.
MANTRA:
GUROO GUROO WAHAY GUROO,
GUROO RAAM DAS GUROO
(As a Servant of the Infinite I Receive His Wisdom)

136

Mudra for Protection

CHAKRA: All Chakras
HEALING COLOR: All Color

Sit with a straight spine. Cross your left hand over your right one and place them on your upper chest. Palms are facing you and all fingers are together. Hold for three minutes and feel the immediate energy shift.
BREATH: Long, deep and slow.
MANTRA: *OM*
(God in His Absolute State)

Mudra for Invisibility

CHAKRA: All Chakras
HEALING COLOR: All Color

Sit with a straight spine and make a fist with your right hand. Lift it to the
level of your solar plexus, the palm facing toward you. Now hold your left
hand above your right fist, palm facing down. The hands are not touching.
Hold for three minutes and relax.
BREATH: Long, deep and slow.
MANTRA: *OM*
(God in His Absolute State)

Mudra for Victory

CHAKRA: All Chakras
HEALING COLOR: All Color

Sit with a straight spine. Make gentle fists with both hands and cross them
in front of your upper chest, left over right.
This Mudra is seen in many sculptures of pharaohs in Egypt.
BREATH: Long, deep and slow.
MANTRA: *OM*
(God in His Absolute State)

Mudra for Evoking Inner beauty

CHAKRA: Solar plexus 3, Heart 4
HEALING COLOR: Yellow, green

Sit with a straight spine and lift your hands in front of your solar plexus.
Interlock the fingers and hold the palms flat and wide open as if displaying
a beautiful flower placed in your hands. Absorb its beauty.
BREATH: Long, deep and slow.
MANTRA: *OM*
(God in His Absolute State)

Mudra for Evoking the Sacred Scent of Perfume

CHAKRA: Heart 4, Throat 5
HEALING COLOR: Green, blue

Sit with a straight spine and lift your right hand to the level between your heart and throat, the palm facing toward the left hand. Lift the left hand and make a fist. With the flat lower part of your fingers, press your fist against the palm of your right hand. Apply gentle pressure and hold.
Higher states of meditation while practicing this Mudra,
will evoke a special magnified sense of sacred scent.
BREATH: Long, deep and slow.
MANTRA: *OM*
(God in His Absolute State)

Mudra for Balancing the Yin and Yang

CHAKRA: All Chakras
HEALING COLOR: All Colors

Sit with a straight spine. Connect the thumbs and index fingers, extending the rest of the fingers and spacing them apart. Lift your right hand up in front of your chest with the palm turned outward, the fingertips pointing left. Hold the left hand below the right in front of your stomach area, palm turned inward and fingertips pointing right. Now connect the thumbs and index fingers of both hands, creating the Wheel of Life.
BREATH: Long, deep and slow.
MANTRA: *OM*
(God in His Absolute State)

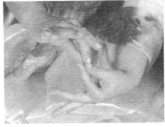

Mudra for Calling the Gods of Earth

CHAKRA: Base of spine 1, Crown 7
HEALING COLOR: Red, violet

Sit with a straight spine. Bend your elbows and place your left hand at your solar plexus, palm facing upward, fingers together. Bring your right hand below your left, palm facing your body, and point the right index finger down toward the Earth.
BREATH: Long, deep and slow.
MANTRA: *OM*
(God in His Absolute State)

Mudra for Evoking the Power of Jupiter

CHAKRA: Heart 4, Throat 5, Third Eye 6
HEALING COLOR: Green, blue, indigo

Sit with a straight spine. Bend the left arm and place the right elbow into the cupped left hand. Make a fist with the right hand and point the index finger up. With the upper part of the right arm, make counterclockwise circles, two revolutions per inhale and two revolutions per exhale. Feel the energy created with your circles.
BREATH: Long, deep and slow.

Mudra for Receiving God's Law

CHAKRA: Crown 7
HEALING COLOR: Violet

Sit with a straight back. Lift the right hand to heart level, palm facing down, and the left hand to your solar plexus area, palm facing up toward the sky. Leave enough space between the palms for a small ball. Elbows are to the side. All fingers are together and straight. Hold the Mudra and concentrate on the energy between your palms.
BREATH: Long, deep and slow.
MANTRA: *OM*
(God in His Absolute State)

145

PART 5.

MUDRA THERAPY SETS
for
SPECIFIC AILMENTS

MUDRA THERAPY SETS FOR SPECIFIC AILMENTS

Mudra Therapy sets are ideal for creating an optimal state of harmony and giving your body the opportunity to heal itself. To help eliminate an ailment, an illness or a disease, I encourage you to take a systematic approach to your healing process. Instead of just wanting the problem to go away as quickly as possible, find the source of your problem and systematically eliminate it forever.

When you are challenged by a physical discomfort, your body is sending you a message. It has been sending you a message for a while, but you have not heard it. Now the message is stronger, louder and more painful. In fact, it is so disturbing that it is impossible to ignore it. Now you have to pay attention. By simply brushing it away, you still have not addressed the cause of the problem. And if you do not, the problem will eventually return. Each time it will return more fiercely and with more power, unhappy that you still have not addressed the deeper cause.

Doesn't all that make it really logical to find the source right away?
Your "search" should be tedious, detail oriented and lovingly patient.
It is an unfortunate fact that we are least patient with ourselves, least loving, taking the least time, and not hearing our inner voice.

No matter what your daily duties are, you need to take care of yourself with attention and clear intention. It is only after you have healed yourself, that you can help others, take care of them, or save the world.

In the following chapters we will address the therapeutic effects of Mudras for various ailments. In each chapter you will also find guidance on how to search and successfully find the cause of your issue by bringing awareness to your emotional state and redirecting your mental monologue. It is your responsibility and choice to make the necessary changes in your lifestyle and assure your physical body the optimal circumstances for healthy functioning.

In addition, you will find instructions on sensory holistic healing modalities that -when combined together with Mudras – magnify and accelerate the positive effects. Mudra Therapy addresses all your senses and creates an open energy filed to speed up your optimal recovery.

HOW TO USE THE MUDRA THERAPY SEQUENCING

In the following pages you will find a wide selection of various Mudra Therapy sequences for specific ailments. Keep in mind that each challenging issue of your health may have many aspects to be considered. For optimal results you may have to practice a few different sequences to cover all areas that need healing. Or, if an illness has given you multiple symptoms, you can use sequences to alleviate as many symptoms as possible. For example; if chronic Lyme disease gives you pain and anxiety, in your specific case, you would add the two sequences for that particular issue to your program.

Offering your body as many tools for self healing and regaining the much needed and desired healthy balance is your goal.

As always keep in mind that all these Mudra Therapy sequences work harmoniously with other healing protocols and always consult with your healthcare provider for optimal care.

Each Mudra Sequence will list the following sensory healing elements, as they should be added to your Mudra Therapy practice protocol.

SENSORY HEALING ELEMENTS

With Mudra Therapy we will engage all your senses to establish an optimal multidimensional space for healing.

TOUCH - FEELING

Mudras are the technique to help you focus on the healing power of touch.

SOUND - HEARING

The effect of sound has most powerful healing aspects. Here you will find a variety of recommended sounds for your condition.

SIGHT - VISUALIZATION

Your capacity to visualize a harmonious environment and healing progress greatly affects the outcome. Here you will find most effective visualization suggestions or visual tools to promote healing. Practicing in nature will offer immediate vibrant and live-healing visual effects.

TASTE – DIET

This is obviously a very powerful sensory element and important aspect of your healing regimen. Here you will find dietary suggestions to speed the healing process. Keep in mind, more demanding and complex individual needs need to be adjusted and fine-tuned by a nutritional specialist.

SMELL- AROMA

The high frequencies of Essential oils create and environment where bacteria and viruses can not thrive. The sense of smell triggers emotional responses and profoundly affects your energy state. Here you will find a few suggested aromatherapy essential oils for you conditions. Of course you may also follow your own personal choices and preferences - the point is to engage the pleasant sense of smell. Aromatherapy oils can be used as simple inhalation from the bottle or cupped hands, diffusion of oil particles in the air, mists, or gentle inhaling from a handkerchief, tissue, cottonball or pillow.

The suggested use with Mudras is to place a drop of oil in your hand, rub both hands together and cup them over your face. Use the Purest Aroma Essential Oils very sparingly and take time to truly absorb and sense individual flavors.

If your skin is very sensitive, you may use high quality aromatherapy candles instead. They will provide healing effects and help you create and nice meditative atmosphere for your Mudra Therapy practice. Air out the room and do not leave candles unattended. I do not suggest practicing with incense as the smoke is not healthy for your intense breathing.

BREATH

This is a very important element in your detoxifying and healing process. Use as depicted with specific Mudras.

LISTENING TO BODY

Here you will find direction for getting in touch with your body, connecting with physical sensations and paying attention to all physical signals sent to you by your body.

FEELINGS - EMOTIONS

You will find instructions for recognizing and connecting with your current dominant emotional state, which will lead you to a deeper understanding of the source of the issues you are dealing with on your emotional level.

MIND AFFIRMATIONS

Affirming and inputting a strong positive mental directive at the moment when you are receptive, presents a wonderful opportunity for eliminating habitual negative mental patterns and changing direction. This is the opportunity for you to take charge of your mindset and become an active participant and not a passive observer. One of the key needed components on your path to healing.

PRACTICE TIME REQUIRED

Follow the suggested time for practice of each sequence to achieve the optimal desired results.

CHAKRA TUNE-UP SET

In this Mudra Chakra tune – up set you will create an overall state of inner harmony and energy balance. When your chakra centers are active, open and properly functioning, you are receptive to healing on numerous subtler dimensions. This is also an excellent health maintenance sequence or a great preparation set before you practice any other more specific Mudra Therapy sequence.

PRACTICE TIME REQUIRED: This is a 31 Minute practice – 3 Minutes for each Mudra, followed by a 10 minute meditation and deep relaxation.

MUDRA for Chakra I.& II. Vitality & Letting Go -page 108

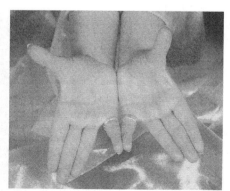

MUDRA for Chakra II.- page 109

MUDRA for Chakra III. - page 110

MUDRA for Healing Your Heart Chakra IV. - page 111

MUDRA for Healing your Voice Chakra V.- page 112

MUDRA for Knowing the Truth Chakra VI. - page 113

MUDRA for Opening Your Crown Chakra VII. - page 114

STRESS and BURN OUT REVERSAL

Everyone in today's world is experiencing stress on some level. The question is: how is this daily stress affecting you? The effects of stress can manifest on various levels, wherever your individual physical system's weakness lies. That means that you could suddenly face digestive issues caused by stress. Or you may suffer from skin disorders - again caused by stress. If the pressure of continued stress causes you to reach a level of general burn-out state of profound and deep exhaustion, your system becomes even more vulnerable to numerous health ailments.

Eliminating stress from your life is not an easy step- the circumstances, relationship and family dynamics and work issues can be complex and challenging to change quickly. But the fact remains that you can honestly expect only a certain amount of time where your body will be able to continuously survive and manage a chronic stressful atmosphere. It may take months or even years before that occurs, but there will come a time when your body will send you serious signals that it has reached it's limits. It is of course best to avoid that accumulated state scenario and with the help of healthy maintenance manage your lifestyle in such a fashion, that you can navigate thru life's up's and down's and remain relatively unaffected. If you have found yourself in a state of burn-out, be for-warned that this is a critical time for you to seriously change your way and do everything possible to regain a state of optimal health. The stress - accumulating phase can go on, but by recognizing a breaking point, you will redirect the set path and rescue yourself from the most common and damaging health threat of our times. Your first step is recognizing the situation- then act. This Mudra Therapy set will help you reverse and heal the effects of burn out and with regular daily practice you will be able to eliminate the damaging effects of stress in your daily life.

SENSORY HEALING ASPECTS:

TOUCH
Mudra sequences as depicted.

SOUND:
Healing musical sounds with calm and gentle tempo, without strong melodies or vocal singing. The sound should be conducive to totally letting

go and not mentally following a melody. Sounds of nature, ocean waves, rain and distant choir. Listening to your breath in silence and stillness.

SIGHT - VISUALIZATION:
Visualize your favorite place in nature, hanging in a hammock looking at the clouds, relaxing without rush, time standing still, floating on the water surface, weightless and free.

TASTE – YOUR DIET: Avoid stress-eating, curb your urges for sugar and junk food to help you alleviate stress - keep in mind it will make matters only worse. Make time for eating in peace, without rush and disturbances. Consciously select foods that best fit your constitution.

SMELL - AROMA:
Encourage deep relaxation in serene environment.
The following essential oils are beneficial:
bergamot, cedar wood, chamomile, cinnamon, clary sage, cypress, frankincense, rose, vetiver, ylang ylang

BREATH:
Use with Mudras as depicted. Long, deep and slow breathing is most beneficial for establishing a stress-free state.

LISTEN TO YOUR BODY:
Pay attention to your body and any areas where physical tension is present. If your stress manifested in physical consequences - focus in that particular area and breathe long, deep and slow while establishing a form of communication with your body.

FEEL YOUR EMOTIONS
Acknowledge your source of stress and emotional connection to it. Writing or voicing your emotions is a form of beneficial release and thus making your emotions far less overwhelming.

YOUR MIND AFFIRMATION:
I am calm, peaceful and relaxed.
I keep my stillness and inner peace at all times.

PRACTICE TIME REQUIRED:
This is a 31 Minute practice. Repeat a sequence combination of choice 3 times. Follow by a few minutes of meditation and deep relaxation.

STRESS AND BURN OUT REVERSAL SET I.

MUDRA for Overcoming Anxiety - page 71

MUDRA for Preventing Burnout - page 72

MUDRA for Preventing Stress - page 74

STRESS AND BURN OUT REVERSAL SET II.

MUDRA for Chakra III. - page 110

Mudra for Preventing Exhaustion - page 120

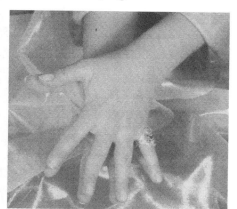

MUDRA for Strength - page 122

IMMUNE SUPPORT

A strong healthy immune system is essential. Many factors affect your immune system and it is important to know that one of it's biggest enemies is stress. Stress is a part of our daily life and a healthy dose of it can stimulate and motivate us. However, when stress is continuous and presents challenges without any relaxation or relief, it turns into distress. Distress has so many damaging effects on your health it is of utmost importance that you regularly work on eliminating that factor from your daily life. If not eliminated, distress can trigger chronic illnesses and numerous serious health conditions. Whatever the cause of your distress, make an effort to remove yourself from the stressful situations or dynamics. Establish a peaceful home environment where you can find relief. Stress puts you into an acidic fight or flight mode. The state of survival becomes your body's main focus and your immune system repair function is put on hold. Your overly acidic state also creates an ideal environment for illness to thrive. Sticking to you basic alkaline diet is even more important if you live with high amounts of stress. This Mudra Therapy sequence will also help you reduce levels of cortisol, a hormone associated with pressure and stress. If your life is a rollercoaster, establish a regular practice routine as a preventative measure.

There are other factors that affect you immune system in a negative way as well; such as pollution, electromagnetic over-saturation and wrong diet, to name a few. Your Immune System is your protector and buffer- every element that jeopardizes its optimal function should be eliminated as much as possible. This is even more important in these times where new viruses are very resilient and can't be easily fought off with conventional medicine. What remains in such a case is your individual resilience and immune system strength. This Mudra Therapy set will help you optimize your Immune System, with regular practice you will remain strong, resilient and adaptive.

SENSORY HEALING ASPECTS:

TOUCH
Mudra sequences as depicted.

SOUND:
Upbeat, energized and happy music of your choice.
Harmonious and easy – nothing aggressive, disturbing or too loud.

SIGHT - VISUALIZATION:
Surround yourself with or visualize your personal favorite serene natural environment, where you can relax and enjoy worry free time.

TASTE – YOUR DIET:
Avoid sugar, acidic foods and all unhealthy foods.
Follow the alkaline diet as much as possible.

SMELL - AROMA:
To promote your body's self healing and cleansing process, you can use essential oils of oregano, rosewood, thyme, lemon, rosemary, and grapefruit.

BREATH:
Short breath of fire is a great detoxifier and stimulant as practiced with Mudra for Trust. Follow with long deep breathing as depicted with other Mudras in sequence for optimal centering and deeply relaxing.

LISTEN TO YOUR BODY:
Be in tune with your body and any signs of discomfort or tension. When you sense an unharmonious area " breathe into it" with intention to let go.

FEEL YOUR EMOTIONS
Acknowledge your feelings and express them. This is the first step in the process of letting go and preventing a congestion of unresolved emotional issues.

YOUR MIND AFFIRMATION:
I radiate health, inner peace and vibrant creative energy.
My body is healthy, strong and protected.

PRACTICE TIME REQUIRED:
This is a 31 Minute practice. Repeat a sequence combination of choice three times. Follow by a few minutes of meditation and deep relaxation.

IMMUNE SUPPORT SET I.

 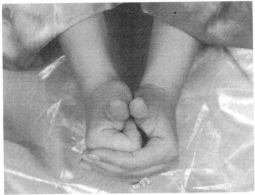

MUDRA for Recharging - page 73

MUDRA for Trust - page 82

MUDRA for Preventing Stress - page 74

IMMUNE SUPPORT SET II.

 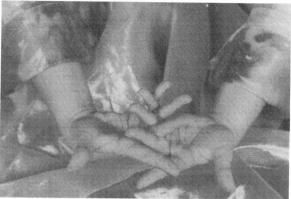

MUDRA for Mental Balance - page 116

MUDRA for Rejuvenation - page 121

MUDRA for Balancing the Yin and Yang - 142

STRONG NERVOUS SYSTEM

A healthy nervous system will help you overcome many challenging circumstances, events or conditions. A weak nervous system can negatively affect various areas of your health and damage your overall wellbeing and quality of life. If you are sensitive, your nervous system will react accordingly when disturbed by environmental elements and sensory overload. It is therefore essential that you establish a nurturing and soothing home environment where you can properly recover and heal your hypersensitivity. If you are exposed to agitation of nervous system on a daily basis, your maintenance regimen has to be disciplined and regular in order to eliminate and prevent further damage to your hyper sensitive state. Pay attention to your environment and use below listed sensory healing elements to preserve and protect the health of your nervous system. In addition to understanding the intimate and close connection between other people's energy and the effect it has on your own energy state, you need to pay specific attention to all possible elements that contribute and elevate your stress levels. Even if you are born with high endurance for stressful and pressured circumstances or professions, you are still susceptible to nervous system damage and burn-out. Your threshold may be higher, but so is your pressure and eventually your limits will be reached. It is much wiser to look ahead and prevent any future long term nervous system damage by consciously selecting a healthier environment. Nobody is invincible, and protecting your nerves ahead of time is a wiser strategy and option. Establishing the current state of your nervous system's overall health is an ongoing process. If you notice a change, like a nervous repetitive action you do or small tremor that happens when you are very tired, pay attention. It is absolutely never too late to reverse the damage and achieve complete recovery. The key is awareness, maintenance and proper daily routine to protect and preserve the healthiest version possible of your nervous system.

SENSORY HEALING ASPECTS:

TOUCH
Mudra sequences as depicted.

SOUND:
Soothing sounds of nature, ocean waves, forest, and rain.

162

SIGHT - VISUALIZATION:
Nature, ocean, forest, clouds, animal life, flowers.

TASTE – YOUR DIET:
Avoid eating spicy, hot and difficult to digest foods.
Select foods that are mild, light, rich in nutrients to minimize the amount of time your body spends digesting them.

SMELL - AROMA:
The best essential oils for improving your nervous system are lavender, neroli, marjoram, ylang-ylang, chamomile, sage, helichrysum.

BREATH:
Breath helps control your emotional states and your emotions affect your breathing. By controlling your breath and practicing deep, slow long breathing, your nervous system has the opportunity to relax and replenish.

LISTEN TO YOUR BODY:
Pay attention to the connection between your physiological state and your various nervous conditions. If under stress, you feel an onset of upset stomach, pay additional attention to help heal and protect these susceptible weaknesses. Furthermore, concentrate on establishing additional peace and stability in these areas.

FEEL YOUR EMOTIONS:
During various times during the day, take a moment and observe your overall state of inner calm or nervous condition. Are you thrown off guard immediately after a minor conflict or challenge, or can you maintain a peaceful disposition amidst chaos? Eliminate emotionally upsetting environments and distance yourself from unharmonious people.

YOUR MIND AFFIRMATION:
I am calm, centered and peaceful. Nothing can disturb my inner anchor of emotional strength and resilience.

PRACTICE TIME REQUIRED:
This is a 31 Minute practice. Repeat a sequence combination of choice three times. Follow by a few minutes of meditation and deep relaxation.

STRONG NERVOUS SYSTEM SET I.

MUDRA for Overcoming Anxiety - page 71

MUDRA for Strong Nerves - page 77

 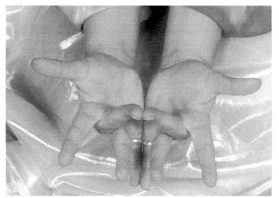

MUDRA for Diminishing Worries - page 97

STRONG NERVOUS SYSTEM SET II.

MUDRA for Strength - page 122

MUDRA For Better Communication
page 130

MUDRA for Activating Third Eye
page 135

OPTIMAL MENTAL HEALTH

As we learned in the Part Two about energy anatomy and cellular memory, the aspect of mental health is complex and all encompassing. Achieving a state of mental health with emotional and behavioral balance is no small task. Each one of us has a set of unique circumstances that perhaps follow us thru life and contribute to who we are. So what is that optimal function where we can assure healthy functioning no matter what environment we are in? Foremost you need to know who you are, why you are the way you are, and how to adapt your unique elements to help you lead a most productive, happy, healthy and harmonious life.

If your childhood was challenging, acknowledge those issues, recognize them and communicate about them. You can not expect to be an emotionally perfectly balanced being without ever communicating your deepest fears or hurtful experiences that left you with some serious scars. If you do not recognize and make peace with your past, you will have a harder time establishing harmony in the present and certainly also in the future. There is no shame in your past for it makes you unique- there is no shame in mistakes you've made because all of us have. Getting in touch with your inner emotional states will help you establish a mental balance, understand yourself, be confident as an individual and reach your fullest potential. Surrounding yourself with loving, encouraging and kind individuals is essential. Recognizing that perhaps you are inclined towards previous dysfunctional patterns or destructive, negative or even addictive company you are repeating the negative pattern that you experienced in the past. Yes, life can be harmonious, happy and pleasant, yes you deserve all the best things life has to offer, and yes it is possible. Communication, self- reflection and honesty are the key components.

If you feel overwhelmed with unresolved mental issues, you need to seek professional help. This Mudra Therapy sets will work in harmony with any other healing modality you are using.

SENSORY HEALING ASPECTS:

TOUCH
Mudra sequences as depicted.

SOUND:
Soothing healing sounds of harp, violin, cheerful upbeat and comforting melodies. No aggressive, depressing or heavy tunes.

SIGHT - VISUALIZATION:
Visualize your "perfect world", where you see yourself happy, healthy and successful in all areas of life. Observe and experience how that feels.

TASTE – YOUR DIET:
Eat a healthy diet, stay away from junk foods, acidic foods, sugar, or too much meat. Often a food allergy or oversensitivity can create a very emotionally sensitive, aggressive, over-reactive and unstable mental state. Make notes of your mental disposition after various foods to find the proper diet for you.

AROMATHERAPY:
Use a wide variety of oils mentioned in previous chapters for: diminishing anxiety, and strengthening the nervous system.

BREATH:
A long, deep and calm breath will always soothe, calm and center your mindset. The breath of fire will establish a nice energy level and help overcome despondent, lethargic and pessimistic demeanor.

LISTEN TO YOUR BODY:
Be still and sense your body, each and every part, from the tip of your toes to the top of your head. Find areas where you sense tension and focus on conscious release with breath.

FEEL YOUR EMOTIONS
Journal work, expressing emotional states, and taking responsibility for your decisions, actions - your mental health is nothing to be lazy about or to procrastinate with. Take action and create conscious positive change.

YOUR MIND AFFIRMATION:
I nurture and love my inner peace and strength.
I voice my feelings, release them and let them go in peace.

PRACTICE TIME REQUIRED:
This is a 31 Minute practice. Repeat a sequence combination of choice three times. Follow by a few minutes of meditation and deep relaxation

OPTIMAL MENTAL HEALTH SET I.

MUDRA for Wisdom - page 86

MUDRA for Happiness - page 94

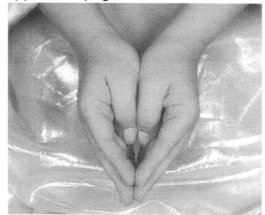

MUDRA for Higher Consciousness - page 100

OPTIMAL MENTAL HEALTH SET II.

MUDRA for Creativity - page 125

MUDRA for Open Heart - page 127

MUDRA for Healthy Eyes - page 133

MEMORY IMPROVEMENT

We live much longer than our ancestors and are well aware of the possibility and dangers of suffering from dementia as we age. The world current statistic say there are 36 Million people living with some kind of dementia. Alzheimer's is a main cause of this staggering numbers. Preventing this illness is much more complex than one imagines and an array of factors play a decisive role in the causes of dementia.

Certainly wrong diet is a major factor. Why? Because by eating sugary and acidic foods we establish an environment in our physical body that is supremely comfortable and inviting to bacteria, virus, fungi and general deterioration of resilience and brain health. We have established now numerous times how damaging the effects of chronic stress are, and yes dementia is one of them. There are other physical dispositions which also create an excellent environment for bacteria to thrive including metal toxicity. And all those elements can not be taken lightly. You may not be able to see any damaging effects for years, but when your immune system weakens with age or a dramatic stressful event in your life occurs; the first sings of dementia will creep up. Forgetfulness, short memory lapses, irritable demeanor, anger outbursts, feeling confused, getting lost or simply not remembering names - those are all signs that you are exhausted and your brain function is suffering. But, you must know that the human brain has incredible elasticity and amazing capacity to regenerate. It means that you absolutely can improve and even recover your memory and brain function, BUT you must take conscious steps and create an optimally healthy environment, diet and activities. The Mudra Therapy sequences will help you keep the brain capacity recharged and energized. Eating a healthy diet and leading a healthy lifestyle with plenty of sleep will most definitely improve and prevent your memory from diminishing. Be disciplined and diligent and remember- cherish your mind and do all you can to protect and preserve its optimal function.

SENSORY HEALING ASPECTS:

TOUCH
Mudra sequences as depicted.

SOUND:
Soothing healing sounds have a positive effect on memory and brain health, as well as active listening or playing an instrument.

SIGHT - VISUALIZATION:
Exercising your mind by retracing your old environments, practicing visual games like chess, crossword puzzles and calculating can be excellent tools for maintaining your brain elasticity.

TASTE – YOUR DIET:
No sugar or acidic foods, eat vibrant fresh foods, drink plenty of water, avoid dehydration, eat healthy fats: coconut oil, extra virgin olive oil, antioxidants, vitamins& minerals, healthy protein and plenty of fiber

AROMATHERAPY:
For memory improvement and alertness: rosemary, cypress, peppermint, basil. For dementia agitation: lemon balm and lavender.

BREATH:
For brain alertness breath of fire, for calming and relaxing long deep and slow breathing technique. Inhaling and counting to 5, holding 5 counts, and exhaling 5 counts, and holding 5 counts. Repeat.

LISTEN TO YOUR BODY:
Be connected with your physical body, become aware when your memory is not as fast as before, immediately create a peaceful environment, get plenty of sleep and healthy nourishment. Notice how quickly you recover- however do not push yourself to this limit too often. This is a signal that you are "pushing the envelope".

FEEL YOUR EMOTIONS
Are you afraid to loose your memory? Become an active participant in preserving and improving your brain health and not a passive victim and observer. Turn your fear and anxiety into focused effort and determination.

YOUR MIND AFFIRMATION:
My mind is sharp, clear, in tune and focused.
My mind is replenished, energized and actively alert. I am present.

PRACTICE TIME REQUIRED:
This is a 31 Minute practice. Repeat a sequence combination of choice three times. Follow by a few minutes of meditation and deep relaxation.

MEMORY IMPROVEMENT SET I.

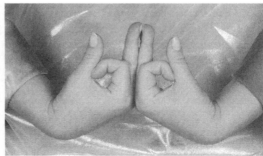

MUDRA for Concentration - page 85

MUDRA for Efficiency - page 90

MUDRA for Calming Your Mind - page 101

MEMORY IMPROVEMENT SET II.

MUDRA for Energy in Upper Chakras - page 107

MUDRA for Uplifting Your Heart - page 106

MUDRA for Brain Synchrony- Readjusting Your Perception - page 134

PAIN MANAGEMENT

If you are in pain, your primary concern is a fast and effective relief. Once that is accomplished, you often tend to forget and ignore the unbalanced elements that caused the pain in the first place. But as we know, a quick pain remedy often won't fix the problem in the long run. Pain is a strong signal from your physical body that you need to pay attention and change your lifestyle. Chronic pain can be debilitating. The symptoms include persistent pain that does not go away after an illness or injury, burning, aching, discomfort, soreness, tightness or stiffness.The causes of chronic pain can be numerous and can be connected to a past injury, arthritis, headache, multiple sclerosis, fibromyalgia or nerve damage. When you suffer from chronic pain, your every function and activity is affected and the comfort of your daily life compromised. Everything seems to revolve around your efforts to minimize the pain, and more often than not you simply accept and live with it. It doesn't have to be so. Deep relaxation has been shown to alter perceptions of pain. Often when we are experiencing pain, we tense up and hold our breath, making pain worse. A cramped up muscle develops into a stiff area, limits your mobility, creates additional discomfort in surrounding areas and eventually your entire body. As a consequence your mental disposition turns negative and your emotional state is affected by permanent discomfort. Pain can turn your daily activities and life in general into a very challenging and unpleasant state. Locating the source of pain and the actual deep cause or reason for onset is of utmost importance. Chronic pain can be connected to nerve inflammation, joint inflammation and that can often be caused by wrong diet. It truly is astonishing how many ailments are connected to that aspect. By following the optimal diet for your specific constitution and applying the following pain management healing modalities, you will alleviate and often eliminate much of chronic pain and discomfort.

SENSORY HEALING ASPECTS:

TOUCH
Mudra sequences as depicted

SOUND:
Soothing music encourages deep relaxation and rest. Use the sounds of nature, ocean, or string instruments to evoke a higher state of consciousness and help disconnect from physical pain.

SIGHT - VISUALIZATION:

With every breath, visualize exhaling pain in a form of gray cloud and visualize inhaling white healing light that is dissolving your pain.

TASTE – YOUR DIET: This sensory stimuli requires much control. Do not seek comfort foods that will increase your pain.
Avoid sugar, acidic foods and all foods that aggravate your condition.
Beneficial diet: whole grains, salmon, ginger, tumeric, strawberries, greens in addition to basic alkaline diet.

SMELL - AROMA:

Encourage relaxation on a deep level that will help you release physical tension and promote peace. The following essential oils are beneficial: lavender, chamomile, marjoram, rosemary, tea tree, cypress, peppermint, eucalyptus, bergamot, geranium

BREATH:

This is a key element for pain management. Long, deep and slow breathing is most beneficial for eliminating chronic pain.
It will help you release tension, anxiety and fear. You will enter a deeply relaxed state where your nervous system will calm down and your pain will subside.

LISTEN TO YOUR BODY:

Pay attention to your body and exact location of pain, so that you may focus on that area with your visualization and slow, deep breath.

FEEL YOUR EMOTIONS

Acknowledge your core feelings and practice Mudras that address your specific needs and help improve your overall emotional state.

YOUR MIND AFFIRMATION:

My body is comfortable, my mind is at peace and calm,
I am deeply relaxed and pain free.

PRACTICE TIME REQUIRED:

This is a 31 Minute practice. Repeat a sequence combination of choice 3 times. Follow by a few minutes of meditation and deep relaxation.

PAIN MANAGEMENT SET I.

MUDRA for Developing Meditation - page 68

MUDRA for Divine Worship - page 69

MUDRA for Tranquilizing Your Mind - page 96

PAIN MANAGEMENT SET II.

MUDRA for Emotional Balance - page 115

MUDRA for Self- Healing - page 119

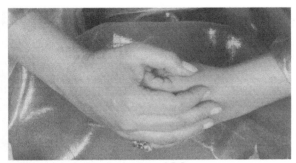

MUDRA for Relaxation and Joy - page 123

ELIMINATING ARTHRITIS AND CARPAL TUNNEL

Those two ailments are of course different, but in regards to holistic therapeutic modalities they require similar remedies and discipline. Since Arthritis dos often manifest in joints of the fingers and hands, Mudras can be of tremendous help to keep the afflicted area flexible and pain free. Carpal tunnel is caused by pressure on the median nerve which can occur because of similar aspects as arthritis in that area. There is no doubt that inflammation plays a decisive role in both of these ailments. That means that proper diet is again supremely important. All foods that cause inflammation must be eliminated. By keeping your system hydrated, properly nourished you will establish optimal circumstances for the inflammation to subside. The next element is maximum oxygenation of your system. The breathing techniques used with Mudras provide ideal opportunity for this additional healing element. Furthermore, the Mudras will help increase and maintain flexibility of your hands, wrists, fingers and arm joints. The least productive thing to do when suffering from this ailment is to become inactive and stay indoors, and eat sugary foods. This will not only maintain the illness but also create ideal circumstances for advancement. You need to become active, conscious about every element of your diet and nutrition and exposure to fresh air, oxygenating your system, and if pain is challenging, gentle swimming will help as well. When you are experiencing pain in your joints and muscle stiffness, the natural response is to tighten and curl up. By remaining disciplined about your healing regimen you will successfully eliminate inflammation and reduce the pain. With regular Mudra practice and application of other Mudra Therapy sensory healing elements you will overcome this illness and retain flexibility and ease of movement in your fingers, hands, wrists and arms.

SENSORY HEALING ASPECTS:

TOUCH
Mudra sequences as depicted.

SOUND:
Light, gently upbeat sounds of nature to stimulate activity and optimistic demeanor. Sounds of ocean, gentle rain, waterfall and forest.
Harp, guitar, chimes, flute and piano.

SIGHT - VISUALIZATION:
Visualize your optimal creative environment where you can pursue your creative talents whatever they may be- stimulating pleasant activity where you are limitless with your capacity and inspiration

TASTE – YOUR DIET:
Avoid any and all foods that create an ideal body environment for inflammation: no sugar, sweets, gluten; keep a diary with your diet and mark how you feel after consuming certain foods so you find your individual preferences for optimal diet plan.

SMELL - AROMA:
The oils used in this case are to relieve joint pain and stiffness and promote relaxation and deep tension relief: eucalyptus, lavender, helichrysum, orange oil, ginger, vanilla

BREATH:
For easing pain and stiffness use long deep breath and consciously breathe into the areas that are most challenged, if your hands are in pain visualize inhaling soothing energy and exhaling all tension; continue with focus for at least 5 minutes at a time

LISTEN TO YOUR BODY:
Be alert and aware of what your body is experiencing, the situations and conditions that worsen your state like cold environment or spicy foods, pay attention and consciously modify trouble causing elements and note improvement

FEEL YOUR EMOTIONS
In stillness and peace explore your core feelings, anything that is unresolved in your far past that is literally emotionally and somewhat physically crippling you in some way. Acknowledge and let go. Make space for new, happy and healthy emotions.

YOUR MIND AFFIRMATION:
I breathe with the sun and am filled with the universal strength and elasticity to adapt to any environment I desire. I am free.

PRACTICE TIME REQUIRED:
This is a 31 Minute practice. Repeat a sequence combination of choice three times. Follow by a few minutes of meditation and deep relaxation.

CARPAL TUNNEL SET I.

MUDRA for Overcoming Anxiety - 71

MUDRA for Prosperity - 87

MUDRA for Inner Security - page 99

ARTHRITIS SET I.

MUDRA for Powerful Energy - page 118

MUDRA for Self- Healing - page 119

MUDRA for Meditation of Change - page 132

CONQUERING FIBROMYALGIA

This ailment creates a complex combination of symptoms that can range anywhere from widespread pain, extreme fatigue, joint stiffness, sleep disturbances, depression, cognitive disorders, numbness and tingling. It is challenging to point to a singular triggering cause however, a disciplined strategy and persistent application of proper combination of healing modalities will help you conquer it and force it into remission. The challenging aspect is when you are faced with a plethora of choices in regards to traditional medications to fight all these numerous symptoms - the danger for overmedicating and completely loosing touch with your actual physical state apart from various side effects becomes more difficult. Therefore I encourage you to truly embark on a self exploratory journey to get to know your physical body, it's likes and dislikes and manage your lifestyle and immediate environment to establish ideal circumstances for comfort and accelerated return to optimal health. It is most important to establish a strong sense of inner peace and patience within yourself. Frustration towards your physical self is not productive – practice self love, inner reflection and careful mindful observation of countless contributors to your state and consequentially your healing. Your attention is required on many realms. This is not something you can ignore or fix in a rushed fashion. Attention to detail, acknowledgement of all emotional states that burden you, frustrations and most importantly all stress contributors must be addressed and eliminated as much as possible. A burned-out state, hyper sensitive organism and chronically stressed out lifestyle can easily trigger this ailment- we again return to basics; healthy alkaline diet, eliminating all possible allergy triggers that cause inner inflammation which a part this ailment. Next: a significant change in lifestyle and emotional circumstances. Mudra Therapy is substantially helpful in establishing this new lifestyle, maintaining a stress -free disposition and oxygenating your system to help subside the inflammation. Stay on course and conquer!

SENSORY HEALING ASPECTS:

TOUCH
Mudra sequences as depicted.

SOUND:
Serene, healing, relaxing, soothing and calming sounds of strings, water elements, birds, slow tempo; conscious listening to melody

SIGHT - VISUALIZATION:
Bathing in warm ocean, lightness of body, healing rays of sun,
flower fields

TASTE – YOUR DIET:
Eat a nutritious and healthy diet, eliminate acidic foods, ALL SUGAR, or
any foods that contribute to your inner inflammation

AROMATHERAPY:
Since the affected areas vary, use corresponding essences: for pain (see
chapter) for stress and anxiety relief: rose, clary sage, sweet orange,
ylang ylang, sandalwood. For sore joints: eucalyptus, peppermint, juniper

BREATH:
Long deep breathing for deep relaxation and release of tension.
Short breath of fire for energizing and recharging
when experiencing deep fatigue and lethargy.

LISTEN TO YOUR BODY:
Concentrate on proper recognition and source of your discomforts and
focus with guided breath on releasing the symptoms
and easing pain or anxiety.

FEEL YOUR EMOTIONS
Voicing feelings as a results of uncomfortable physical conditions, focus
on releasing despondent states, open up the capacity to receive healing
love into your heart. Forgive and let go.

YOUR MIND AFFIRMATION:
I am empowering my body to heal with love and light.
I am healing, I am recharged, I am free.

PRACTICE TIME REQUIRED:
This is a 31 Minute practice. Repeat a sequence combination of choice
three times. Follow by a few minutes of meditation and deep relaxation.

CONQUERING FIBROMYALGIA SET I.

MUDRA for Taking Away Hardship - page 92

MUDRA for Contentment - page 95

MUDRA for Anti aging - page 78

CONQUERING FIBROMYALGIA SET II.

MUDRA for Lower Spine - page 102

MUDRA for Middle Spine - page 103

MUDRA for Upper Spine - page 104

OVERCOMING LYME

This is an extremely complex and challenging illness called "the great imitator". The symptoms of this illness are so wide reaching and imitate so many other illnesses it creates an incredibly complex puzzle. Sufferers may develop very different symptoms, making it challenging to properly diagnose. Lyme - also known as Lyme Borreliosis, was named after a small town on the east Coast of USA, but can be found around the world. Lyme can be transmitted thru infected bites from a tick, mosquito, horse fly and other biting insects. An infection can occur without an allergic reaction to the insect bite, simply in form of a bad flu. There are currently complex battles going on regarding proper treatment since the prescribed treatment after a Lyme infection is usually just a three week dose of antibiotics. However, that does often not suffice. It is a good beginning, but Lyme bacteria are incredibly sophisticated and remain in your system forever. About 95% of population have this virus in their system, BUT it will not manifest unless the conditions are perfect. What are these perfect conditions? As usual - a weakened immune system. This can happen with older age, at onset of another illness, accident or extremely stressful event. The illness will manifest differently depending on the individual's weaknesses and predispositions. It may manifest in the form of autoimmune disorders, Lupus or even infertility, inflammatory bowel disease, arthritis or rheumatism, or neuro-borreliosis - with serious memory and cognitive impairment. Lyme disease that is chronic - meaning it is in person's system for years undiscovered, may often cause serious illness like: Dementia, Bi-polar disorders, Chronic Fatigue syndrome, Fibromyalgia, Alzheimer's, Parkinson's, Multiple sclerosis, and more. Lyme is incredibly challenging to diagnose since the conventional tests perform very poorly. It is also possible for the bacteria to go dormant and if one is tested at that time, the results will most likely be negative. This illness is very serious, but can be managed with good care of a specialist, especially when caught early at the onset. It is more challenging to deal with it once it has set into a chronic pattern and has continuously challenged a particular aspect of your health in a more serious way. Herbal and natural remedies can be extremely helpful as well as holistic frequency technologies. Mudra Therapy is ideal technique for sufferers, because Lyme bacteria, retrieves into a dormant state when your body is strongly oxygenated. Mudra Therapy establishes this oxygenated state that helps control the illness and prevents flare-ups.

SENSORY HEALING ASPECTS:
TOUCH
Mudra sequences as depicted.
SOUND:
Soothing healing sounds of ocean, very gentle meditative music,
soft melodies, rain
SIGHT - VISUALIZATION:
Fill your entire body with glowing light, scan each body part in detail and
visualize healing every cell. Focus on affected area -often entire body -
and cool down inflamed sore areas with visuals of waterfall & soothing rain
TASTE – YOUR DIET:
Eat a nutritious but bland diet, avoid spices, absolutely no sugar, too many
carbs or meat. No acidic foods where Lyme bacteria thrives. Create a very
specialized menu for your needs avoiding all inflammatory elements.
AROMATHERAPY:
For reducing inflammation: lavender, peppermint, helichrysum, nutmeg,
balsam and white fir, wintergreen. For calm sleep: lavender, jasmine,
chamomile, valerian

BREATH:
Conscious long deep breathing into affected areas and exhaling toxic
inflamed sensation replacing it with a cooling healing breath.

LISTEN TO YOUR BODY:
High awareness of all conditions that affect you negatively. Disciplined
daily routine to create an ideal setting for absolute peace and calm

FEEL YOUR EMOTIONS
Feelings of helplessness need to be replaced with hope, optimism,
strength, confidence and much self-love.
Deserving and claiming the right to perfect health.

YOUR MIND AFFIRMATION:
My absolute harmonious health is my birthright.
I love myself unconditionally and deserve happiness.
I am winning, overcoming obstacles and am healing.

PRACTICE TIME REQUIRED:
This is a 31 Minute practice. Repeat a sequence combination of choice
three times. Follow by a few minutes of meditation and deep relaxation

OVERCOMING LYME SET I.

MUDRA for Protecting Your Health - page 76

MUDRA for Guidance - page 84

MUDRA for Powerful Insight - page 89

OVERCOMING LYME SET II.

MUDRA for Reproductive Center - page 124

MUDRA for Finding Perfect Truth - page 131

MUDRA for Victory - page 139

FIGHTING OFF CANCER

Cancer is a dreadful disease and just the word alone has a powerful negative effect on our psyche. It is filled with anger, fear, and sadness. BUT, there are many, many cancer survivors who successfully overcame this illness and lead happy productive lives for many years to come. When you are faced with this diagnosis, your world changes. Matters that were important before instantly fade and your perception of what is important crystallizes. As with any illness that carries within the option of no return this one has us facing the worst fears and darkest hours. It is unproductive to compare which illness is worse than the other- all illnesses are difficult in different ways as we are all different. The key element in your fight thru cancer is to eliminate it and prevent it from ever coming back. Whatever medical methods you select, dealing with the key components that played a role in you getting this illness need to be removed. The search is on. The selected Mudras can help you reconnect with the Universal energy that resides in us all, so that you can remember that your spirit is immortal and indestructible. The fear of death can be transformed into awareness that your spirit is unbreakable and ever powerful. The Mudra for help with a grave situation will help you lift your spirits up.The Mudra of love will reactivate the Self-love within you, which is an essential part in your recovery process. As we learned in Part Two about energy anatomy, we discussed how unresolved negative emotions create clusters of negative energy that can materialize into unharmonious diseased matter. Mudra for releasing negative emotions is excellent for resolving unhappy emotional states stemming from your past, letting go, and maintaining a clear energy field. The Mudra for preventing exhaustion will help you thru the healing process which requires stamina, perseverance and much energy. And Mudra for protection will help you fight off and prevent negative energy from overwhelming and overpowering your body. It will help you maintain a protected energy field, so that you can successfully fight off and preserve your health far into the future. Stay steady on your practice and empower yourself with energy to fight and win this battle and emerge victorious, reborn, renewed and elevated.

SENSORY HEALING ASPECTS:
TOUCH
Mudra sequences as depicted.

SOUND:
Soothing healing sounds of string instruments, chimes, kalimba, xylophone and sounds of nature

SIGHT - VISUALIZATION:
Recall personal past state of complete health and happiness – reconstruct the feeling and practice visualizing yourself again happy, Healthy, and completely whole.

TASTE – YOUR DIET:
Eat a nutritious and healthy diet, reduce amount of acidic foods. Eliminate sugar to starve cancer cells and choose all organic nutrients instead.

AROMATHERAPY:
Do not apply to skin. Gently shortly inhale the oils for various needs: for pain (see pain management) for anxiety (see diminishing fear and anxiety), also: frankincense, lemongrass, thyme and oregano

BREATH:
Most of your body's toxins are released thru exhalation. Therefore your concentration on proper long and deep breathing is more important than ever. Long deep breathing for soothing, calming down and relaxing, releasing tension and pain management.

LISTEN TO YOUR BODY:
Be body conscious, register various elements that may be out of harmony. Pay attention to your physical condition and eliminate unnecessary discomforts or strain. Be kind to your body.

FEEL YOUR EMOTIONS
It is imperative to acknowledge your current emotional state and release emotions you do not want to carry with you - then consciously with focus release and replace them with loving, happy and healthy emotions

YOUR MIND AFFIRMATION:
I am calm, centered and peaceful. My inner anchor of emotional strength and resilience is undisturbed. I am healing victoriously.

PRACTICE TIME REQUIRED:
This is a 31 Minute practice. Repeat a sequence combination of choice three times. Follow by a few minutes of meditation and deep relaxation.

FIGHTING OFF CANCER SET I.

MUDRA for Universal Energy and Eternity - page 70

MUDRA for Help with a Grave Situation - page 75

MUDRA for Love - page 83

FIGHTING OFF CANCER SET II.

MUDRA for Releasing Negative Emotions - page 117

MUDRA for Preventing Exhaustion - page 120

MUDRA for Protection - page 137

DIMINISHING FEAR AND ANXIETY

Fear is a very decisive factor in your overall health and energy state. The effects can spread and negatively affect numerous dynamics in your life. Eventually a basic deep fear can prevent important life progress and when left unaddressed it creates a state of illness and disharmony in various areas. Fear affects mental, emotional and physical body in an unproductive and energy blocking way. Fear is always worse when not faced and dealt with. It becomes a stronger disturbing element. Facing your fears is most beneficial and often produces instant release. As a result, a positive change follows like a chain reaction. All fears stem from basic fear of death - this make sense, since we humans are chronically afraid of everything and anything we do not fully understand, know about, or can tangibly touch. Past trauma can also cause fears; fear of being hurt, loosing respect, suffering in loneliness, falling on hard times, helplessness - there are what it seems never-ending possibilities for fearful states. It cripples your progress, movement forward, possibilities of achieving your dreams, experiencing happiness, success and love. Fear is very closely connected to regret. Whenever fear prevented you from taking advantage of an amazing opportunity, almost instantly regret follows. Now, we live with the fear in addition to regret. Fear also closely attracts anger - we become angry at anyone or ourselves for not being able to face and conquer the fear. Anxiety is a close relative of fear, a state where we are really afraid, but are less likely to recognize our fear - we believe we have just anxiety (less threatening sounding than fear somehow) - yet it is almost like a phase of fear. The fact is that everyone certainly has fears, but everyone would also be better without them. Fearlessness holds no guarantees - it is a risk, and sometimes we do get hurt as a result. Fears are acceptable in small doses where they do not ruin the chances of a happy and healthy life.

An anxiety attack can spoil a perfectly wonderful opportunity before it even has a chance to breathe - a small dose of anxiety can be fine - it can give us a small injection of adrenaline so we can excel at a given decisive moment. The key is managing all our states in a healthy way, so that they benefit us and not hinder us. Talking about fears is good as long as this does not chronically continue in an obsessive way. Then, fear has become a crutch, an excuse for avoiding taking responsibilities for your actions and decisions. Mudra Therapy is an excellent tool to stop the obsessive fear-repetition or anxiety-affirming state, and change the thinking pattern and emotional disposition - altogether successfully diminishing both.

SENSORY HEALING ASPECTS:

TOUCH
Mudra sequences as depicted.

SOUND:
Soothing melodies, violin, slow tempo, sound of cheerful, happy tunes.
No drums, fast or aggressive songs. Classical melodies, sounds of nature.

SIGHT - VISUALIZATION:
Calm lake and water surface, clouds in the sky, flowers opening,
sunshine, walking by the ocean on a sunny carefree day, tracing footsteps

TASTE – YOUR DIET:
Avoid spicy foods and meat. Do not eat too late or get dehydrated.

AROMATHERAPY:
Best scents: grapefruit, bergamot, clary sage, roman chamomile, vetiver,
lavender, sandalwood, juniper, neroli, geranium

BREATH:
Long deep breath, begin with inhalation thru the nose and exhalation thru
the mouth and gradually also exhale with mouth closed, breathing only
thru the nose. Focus on long extended exhalations.

LISTEN TO YOUR BODY:
Observe where in your body the anxiety or fear is centered and
consciously breathe into that area and release with each exhalation.

FEEL YOUR EMOTIONS
Ask yourself what are you afraid off and search for deeper source of your
fears. Acknowledge but do not hold on, confidently release, move forward.

YOUR MIND AFFIRMATION:
*I release my fears and am fearless, protected,
loved and eternally safe.*

PRACTICE TIME REQUIRED:
This is a 31 Minute practice. Repeat a sequence combination of choice
three times. Follow by a few minutes of meditation and deep relaxation.

DIMINISHING FEAR AND ANXIETY SET I.

MUDRA for Facing Fear - page 81

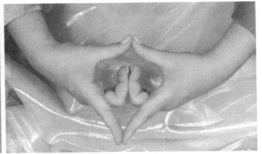

MUDRA for Self-Confidence - page 93

MUDRA for Prosperity - page 87

DIMINISHING FEAR AND ANXIETY SET II.

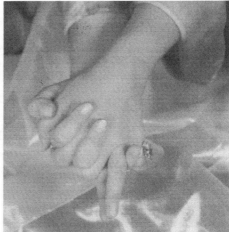

MUDRA for Powerful Energy - page 118

MUDRA of Two Hearts - page 128

MUDAR of Invisibility - page 138

ELIMINATING ADDICTIONS

Addictions come in many forms: drugs, alcohol, smoking, sex, food, gambling, computer, work, shopping, hoarding, dramatic states and chaos, dysfunctional relationships, abuse, violence, competition, dieting, negativity and other troubling versions. When you loose control of your mind, body and emotions, and became enslaved to a physical or psychological addiction you loose freedom, quality of life and eventually yourself in the process. Everything revolves around the addiction, justifying, making excuses, blaming others, lying to others and yourself –it becomes your pattern and crutch. Eliminating addictions is a process that requires involved exploration of all your conditions: physical, emotional, mental, energetic and spiritual. Realizing the uniqueness of your life, the limitless opportunities presented, the vast field of possibilities and the joy of living, is a key inspirational component to regain your healthy state and never allow addictions to take over your precious life again. The escape that the addictive behavior provides is temporary and yet it requires your complete attention. Exploring your deep emotional states on all levels, and finding the hidden void you are so desperately trying to fill up, cover and hide - that is your key to recovery. The imbalance can be harmonized and eliminated. The environment plays a large role, your company, relationships and your lifestyle – if you live in an environment that enables your addictive behavior, you need to change it and remove yourself from all negative influences. Understanding the long term damaging effects to your energy-auric field is also of importance, as the self-destructive behavior is not without long term consequences. The ultimate element in recovery is your personal re-connection with God, Universal power that protects and guides us. Mudra Therapy can be a very powerful healing element in your recovery – disciplined practice helps you establish a state of deep inner peace, serenity and calmness, so you may activate your inner strength to overcome addictive impulses and replace them with new healthy and positive habits.

SENSORY HEALING ASPECTS:

TOUCH
Mudra sequences as depicted.

SOUND:
Soothing sounds of nature to release restlessness, Tibetan bowls

SIGHT - VISUALIZATION:
Visualize yourself on beautiful serene private island where you can rest and surround yourself with only healing elements and activities, swimming in ocean, standing under a gentle waterfall, relaxing in the sun, feeling a gentle breeze. Travel here with your mind when you feel overwhelmed.

TASTE – YOUR DIET:
Food allergies and intolerance can create cravings and imbalances that lead to addictions - therefore diet is crucially important and needs to be professionally adjusted to your individual needs. Eliminate sugar, junk food, gluten & stimulants. Eat in moderation - a variety of organic foods.

AROMATHERAPY:
Applied for cleansing, regaining control and withdrawal of symptoms: Lemon, cedarwood, eucalyptus, clary sage, lavender, melissa, vetiver, ylang ylang, rose, sandalwood

BREATH:
Breath of fire can be an excellent tool to eliminate the need for a substance - it can create a powerful naturally charged state that replaces the need for addictive habit or activity. Follow up with deep, calm breath.

LISTEN TO YOUR BODY:
Regain your connection with your body and do not shut it out- bring awareness into each area step by step from toes to top of your head and search for tense areas that are pushing you into negative habit. Gently relax the area and breathe, establish a deeply relaxed state.

FEEL YOUR EMOTIONS
Recognize what emotional & physical states push you into addictive behavior - use a journal and search further - what dynamics or situations trigger these states – now you have a basic map to healing - use it.

YOUR MIND AFFIRMATION:
I surrender to God's will and ask for healing of my imperfections, and conscious power to carry it thru.

PRACTICE TIME REQUIRED:
This is a 31 Minute practice. Repeat a sequence combination of choice three times. Follow by a few minutes of meditation and deep relaxation.

ELIMINATING ADDICITIONS SET I.

MUDRA for Sexual Balance - page 79

MUDRA for Stronger Character - page 88

MUDRA for Inner security - page 99

ELIMINATING ADDICTIONS SET II.

MUDRA for Opening Your Heart Center - page 126

MUDRA for Empowering Your Voice - page 129

MUDRA for Taking You out of Danger - page 136

HEALTHY WEIGHT

A healthy body is a luxury. Most of receive that gift at birth. Consequently life's events, circumstances and predispositions expose our physical weaknesses and we need to adapt and make some changes. With time your body will reveal consequences of poor diet, unhealthy lifestyle and stress, by show signs of poor health and expedited aging. The key element in maintaining optimal physical health is your diet. Paying attention to what you consume requires discipline and correct approach. Simply starving will not make you healthy and thin. It could make you very unhealthy and can be seriously damaging. Eating healthy also does not have to be expensive. Eating smart and correct for your specific body type is the key. Regular elimination is also very important and needs attention. Curbing your stress and emotional hunger and avoiding succumbing to visual stimuli requires strength and discipline. Many people who battle weight problems don't eat too much - they just eat completely wrong foods for their specific body type and metabolism. They often remain hungry, regularly exercise and still carry around all that excess weight. This results in them giving up the efforts, since they don't seem to have a positive effect. They eventually succumb to emotional comfort eating. By properly changing the diet and eating habits, most everyone can enjoy a healthy physique that will positively affect their view of themselves and life. Explore healthy foods in the Alkaline food group that appeal to you and completely eliminate your carbohydrates and sugar for a while - observe the results. If positive, you may be on the right track. If not, eliminate too much meat or dairy. Do not eat past 7pm, stay away from sugar, all junk food, drink plenty of water with lemon to detoxify, and exercise a gentle regimen. Get in touch with your feelings and observe your emotional state when you feel most hungry. Replace the usual comfort foods with fresh vegetable snacks. When stressed and very emotional, cortisol creates a spike in your appetite. Learn to de-stress daily and establish emotional harmony and inner peace. The following Mudra therapy sequences will help you achieve that.

SENSORY HEALING ASPECTS:
TOUCH
Mudra sequences as depicted.

SOUND:
Calming, relaxing and melodious music, gentle string instruments, chimes

SIGHT - VISUALIZATION:
See your body healthy at ideal weight and sense all the energy you have.
Visualize all the positive effects this change creates for you
and see them come to realization

TASTE – YOUR DIET:
Avoid eating when stressed, eating late or comfort eating.
Follow the alkaline diet, reduce carbohydrates and drink water with lemon.
Replace the stress eating with a healthy snack of fresh vegetable or fruit

SMELL - AROMA:
The best appetite suppressing essential oils are grapefruit, bergamot,
sage, cumin, dill, fennel, ginger, lemon, patchouli, peppermint,
sandalwood, and Ylang Ylang

BREATH:
Breath helps control your emotional states and will help curb your appetite
or emotional eating. You can use long deep breathing or breath of fire.

LISTEN TO YOUR BODY:
Pay attention and learn to differentiate between physical hunger or anxiety
driven hunger. Learn to stop eating when full.
Select light fresh and vibrant foods that energize you.
Prepare your food yourself with love, appreciation and intention.

FEEL YOUR EMOTIONS
Recognize your emotional states that prompt your hunger and urges to eat
especially later in the evening. Eliminate the triggers for stress eating-
establish a calming Mudra Therapy practice time instead.

YOUR MIND AFFIRMATION:
I enjoy eating healthy foods and prepare my meals with loving care.
My body is healthy, beautiful and I select only the best foods for it.

PRACTICE TIME REQUIRED:
This is a 31 Minute practice. Repeat a sequence combination of choice
three times. Follow by a few minutes of meditation and deep relaxation.

HEALTHY WEIGHT SET I.

MUDRA for Help with Diet - page 80

MUDRA for Inner Integrity - page 91

MUDRA for Patience - page 98

HEALTHY WEIGHT SET II.

MUDRA for Activating the Lower Chakras - page 105

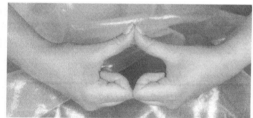

MUDRA for Meditation of Change - page 132

MUDRA for Evoking Inner Beauty - page 140

BALANCING
IRRITABLE BOWEL SYNDROME

This condition has gained much attention in recent years. The many toxic external factors that affect our system seem to have created more challenging circumstances for IBS sufferers. The mind – body and brain – gut connection is a clear element to be taken into consideration when healing this unharmonious state. The many symptoms create a challenging situation that affects all levels of one's life: physical, mental and emotional. Very often it is chronic stress that triggers this ailment and when left unaddressed, the issues become serious. IBS requires strict focus on your diet, eliminating all possible allergies to various substances and foods and establishing a new healthy balance in the intestinal tract. Stress needs to be removed and great discipline is needed to stick to the best diet plan. Often this eliminates carbohydrates, gluten, wheat or grains, sugar, raw foods, greasy foods, meat, dairy and spicy foods. The best diet to heal an acute case of IBS is gentle cooked vegetable soups, warm liquids, small portions, and limited intake of the same foods – any food in excess becomes an irritant. Organic coconut oil can be very helpful in relieving bouts of constipation and warm gentle carrot soups and some protein can help ease the diarrhea. Extreme discipline is required to balance the irritated condition and maintain it going forward. Mudra Therapy is extremely helpful for providing strong support to ease tension, eliminate stress and worry. Explore and remain diligent when re-discovering tolerated foods and eventually you will find a regimen that fits you well and helps you balance this condition and thus eliminate it. Once IBS has developed into a chronic condition, it is most important that you do not slip into bad eating habits again as soon as you feel better. The diet regimen is something your should always stick to with minimal deviations. Do not ignore IBS in beginning phases, it will persist and worsen until you pay attention. On a positive note, with a disciplined diet, you will regain your overall health, maintain ideal weight, and balance your emotional life.

SENSORY HEALING ASPECTS:
TOUCH
Mudra sequences as depicted.

SOUND:
Soothing healing sounds of harp, violin, cheerful upbeat and comforting melodies. No aggressive, depressing or heavy tunes.

SIGHT - VISUALIZATION:

Visualize yourself in a place of complete serenity, surrounded by healing colors of the rainbow. See your body float thru all colors of the charkas and end up surrounded by white healing light, glowing and protecting you.

TASTE – YOUR DIET:

In acute cases: warm cooked vegetables and soups, pureed food, small portions, eating in peace. Regular maintenance: no gluten, carbohydrates, heavy meats, greasy foods, wheat or grains, sugar or junk foods, raw foods, dairy, sweet fruits, or hard crackers. Avoid all possible food irritants or excess of one kind of food. Diligent discipline is needed.

AROMATHERAPY:

Use a wide variety of oils mentioned in chapters for inner peace, diminishing anxiety and strengthening the nervous system.

BREATH:

A long, deep and calm breath will always help you ease the pain or discomfort. Focus on breath and when needed count as you go along to help you achieve deeper calm.

LISTEN TO YOUR BODY:

Pay attention to your stress levels and avoid them at all costs. Do not forget about your food sensitivities when feeling better or allow sliding back into bad eating habits. Keep on track.

FEEL YOUR EMOTIONS

This is the time to recognize the extra burdens you have not addressed, the worries, stress or emotional unresolved issues that are creating this strong imbalance. Acknowledge, find the source and eliminate distress.

YOUR MIND AFFIRMATION:

I love and respect my body and it's needs for proper nutrition. I feed it lovingly and with care, so it can house my spirit comfortably.

PRACTICE TIME REQUIRED:

This is a 31 Minute practice. Repeat a sequence combination of choice three times. Follow by a few minutes of meditation and deep relaxation

BALANCING IRRITABLE BOWEL SYNDROME I.

MUDRA for Help with a Grave Situation - page 75

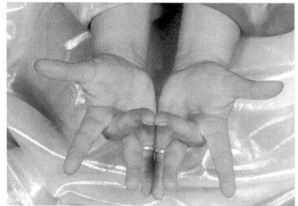

MUDRA for Diminishing Worries - page 97

MUDRA for Calming Your Mind - page 101

BALANCING IRRITABLE BOWEL SYNDROME II.

MUDRA for Emotional Balance - page 115

MUDRA for Mental Balance - page 116

MUDRA for Relaxation and Joy - page 123

OVERCOMING SLEEPLESSNESS

Sleep is an essential element needed for your optimal healthy physical, emotional and mental function. This is the time where your physical and energy body can replenish and recharge on many deeper levels. When sleeplessness is continuous and turns into insomnia, it presents a deeper problem. Unfortunately in such a case the majority of people quickly turn to sleeping medications and become dependant on them. This creates another problem and does not address the core issue. Most often sleeplessness and difficulty falling asleep is a direct result of stress and anxiety. Late night eating habits, incorrect diet also play a role. Another aspect is electromagnetic pollution, which some people are very sensitive to. Sleeping with a mobile phone or computer turned on or too close to bedroom may be enough of a reason to be unable to fall asleep. Another energy pollutants are electronic modems, electric outlets and any electronic instrument that remains turned on at night. Bad placement of bed - under the window - across from a mirror, or directly facing the door with your feet is considered a bad sleeping arrangement in the art of feng shui. What is most important is also your bedtime routine; going to bed always at the same time, taking a warm quick shower before bedtime and following a calming regimen is of outmost importance. Hanging on the phone or falling asleep in front of TV is not favorable. You should create an optimal relaxing bedtime routine that you follow regularly. Mudra Therapy is an excellent technique to help you establish a clam sense of body, mind and emotions while connecting with spirit attunement and establishing a state of deep relaxation before sleep-time. Following meditation, immediately turn off the lights and continue the relaxed state into sleep mode. Personal relationships especially with sleeping partners need to have a harmonious dynamic before bedtime. Simple breathing exercise with counting equal counts for inhalation and exhalation will successfully soothe and relax you into a state of deep rest and rejuvenating sleep. Create an inviting and comfortable sleeping situation.

SENSORY HEALING ASPECTS:

TOUCH
Mudra sequences as depicted.

SOUND:
Soothing sound of calming ocean waves, lullaby of distant angelic choir, harp, soft raindrops, soft piano in higher register, very low volume

SIGHT - VISUALIZATION:

Visualize lying in a hammock by the sea, listening to gentle ocean waves in the distance, inhale and exhale with each wave, softly

TASTE – YOUR DIET:

In the evening eat a light meal not later than 7pm, stay away from heavy meat, too much sugar or excessive alcohol. First thing in the morning drink a glass of warm water with a touch of lemon. Keep your system as clean as possible- alkaline diet recommended.

AROMATHERAPY:

Place a cotton ball next to your bed with a few drops of lavender or chamomile oil. These essences may also be used in mildly warm bath before sleep. Hot bath not recommended.

BREATH:

In your mind count to 5 for inhalation, hold for count of 5, exhale for count of 5 and hold again for count of 5. Repeat. Find the perfect comfortable tempo for you, and continue until you fall asleep.

LISTEN TO YOUR BODY:

Connect with each body part, when exhaling consciously relax that area, release and let go. If you discover tension in an area, mentally spend more time in that region concentrating on release with breath. Patiently continue until connecting with all areas of your body.

FEEL YOUR EMOTIONS

This is the time where you want to calm down and not re-analyze all matters that upset you. It is time for rest and no matter what you are dealing with, consciously concentrate on allowing your body to get the rest it needs. Self love and trust is your focus to help you let go and relax.

YOUR MIND AFFIRMATION:

I am protected, I am loved, I deserve a wonderful deeply relaxing night's sleep and will wake up refreshed and clear in mind and spirit.

PRACTICE TIME REQUIRED:

This practice can be adjusted to your immediate needs. If you begin to feel deeply relaxed, listen to your body's signal, turn off the lights and go to sleep. If you wake up in the night, you may practice again until needed.

OVERCOMING SLEEPLESSNESS I.

MUDRA for Developing Meditation - page 68

MUDRA for Trust - page 82

MUDRA for Contentment - page 95

OVERCOMING SLEEPLESSNESS II.

MUDRA for Opening Your Crown - page 114

MUDRA for Protection - page 137

MUDRA for Rejuvenation - page 121

ABOUT THE AUTHOR

Internationally best-selling author SABRINA MESKO Ph.D.H. has gained a worldwide audience with her book Healing Mudras - Yoga for your hands by Random House. The book reached number five on the Los Angeles Times Health Books Bestseller list and is translated into 14 languages. Sabrina authored more than 20 books on Mudras, Meditation, Yoga and Healing and directed and produced her latest double DVD titled Chakra Mudras – a Visionary awards finalist.

Sabrina studied with Master Guru Maya, healing breath techniques with Master Sri Sri Ravi Shankar and completed a four-year study of Paramahansa Yogananda's Kriya Yoga technique. She graduated from the internationally known Yoga College of India and became a certified yoga therapist.

An immense interest and study of powerful hand gestures - Mudras, led Sabrina to the world's only Master of White Tantric Yoga, Yogi Bhajan, who entrusted her with the sacred Mudra - hand yoga techniques, giving her the responsibility to spread this ancient and powerful knowledge world wide.

Sabrina holds a Bachelors Degree in Sensory Approaches to Healing, a Masters in Holistic Science and a Doctorate in Ancient and Modern Approaches to Healing from the American Institute of Holistic Theology. She is board certified from the American Alternative medical Association and American Holistic Health Association.

Sabrina appeared on The Discovery Channel documentary on hands, the Roseanne Show, CNBC News and numerous international live television programs. Her articles and columns have been published in countless publications. Sabrina has hosted her own weekly TV show about health, well-being and complementary medicine. She is an executive member of the World Yoga Council and has led extensive Teacher Training Yoga Therapy educational programs.

Sabrina has also created award winning international Spa and Wellness Centers from concept, complete with unique healing signature Spa treatments. She is a motivational keynote conference speaker addressing large audiences all over the world. Her highly dynamic and engaging approach leaves audiences inspired and uplifted.

Sabrina lives in Los Angeles.

For more information about her online personal mentorship courses for MUDRA TEACHER TRAINING and MUDRA THERAPY, visit her website: **www.sabrinamesko.com**

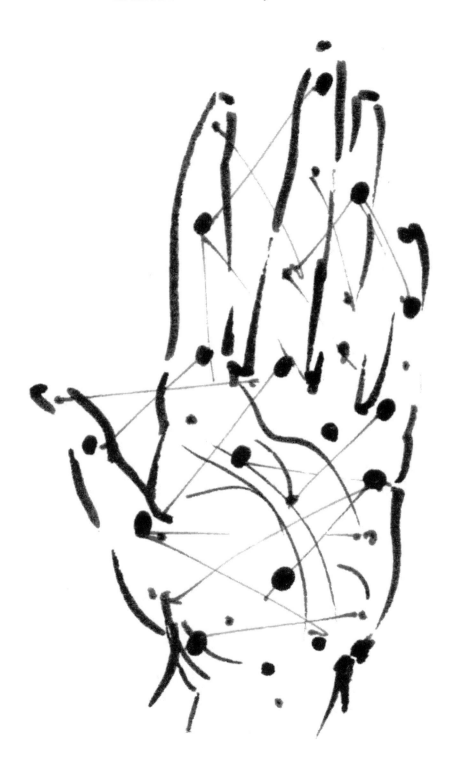

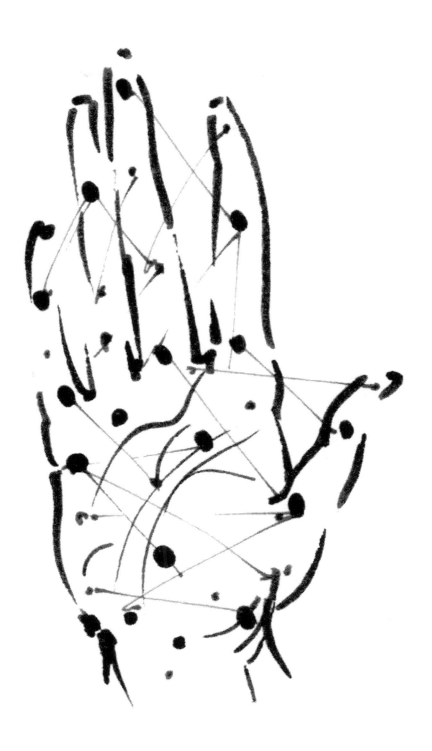

Made in the USA
Middletown, DE
15 September 2017